D1257985

THE AGE OF REVOLUTION

# REVOLUTION AND INDEPENDENCE IN LATIN AMERICA

## THE LIBERATORS

EDITED BY
MEREDITH DAY

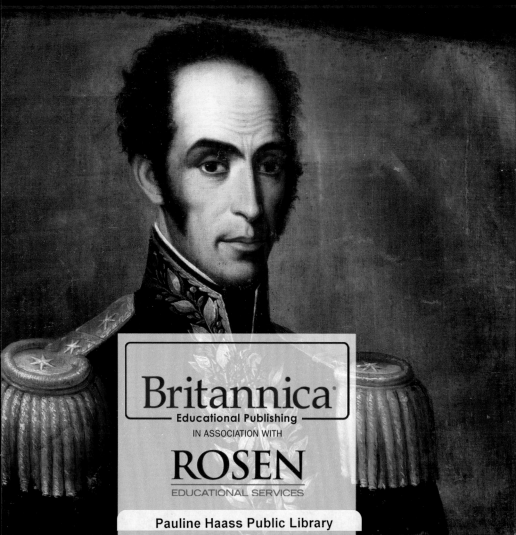

Britannica®
Educational Publishing

IN ASSOCIATION WITH

ROSEN
EDUCATIONAL SERVICES

Published in 2016 by Britannica Educational Publishing (a trademark of Encyclopædia Britannica, Inc.) in association with The Rosen Publishing Group, Inc.
29 East 21st Street, New York, NY 10010

Distributed exclusively by Rosen Publishing.
To see additional Britannica Educational Publishing titles, go to rosenpublishing.com.

First Edition

**Britannica Educational Publishing**
J. E. Luebering: Director, Core Reference Group
Anthony L. Green: Editor, Compton's by Britannica

**Rosen Publishing**
Hope Lourie Killcoyne: Executive Editor
Meredith Day: Editor
Nelson Sá: Art Director
Nicole Russo: Designer
Cindy Reiman: Photography Manager
Supplementary material by Jacob R. Steinberg

**Library of Congress Cataloging-in-Publication Data**

Revolution and independence in Latin America : the liberators/edited by Meredith Day.—First edition.
       pages cm.—(The age of revolution)
   Includes bibliographical references and index.
   ISBN 978-1-68048-029-0 (library bound)
   1. Latin America—History—19th century. 2. Nationalism—Latin America—History—19th century. 3. Latin America—History—Wars of Independence, 1806–1830. I. Day, Meredith.
   F1412.R475 2016
   980'.02—dc23

                                                                              2014040497

*Manufactured in the United States of America.*

# CONTENTS

# CONTENTS

# CONTENTS

# CONTENTS

# CONTENTS

The cultural region today known as Latin America spans roughly 6,000 miles (9,700 kilometers) from the Rio Grande in the north along the United States–Mexico border to the Patagonian islands of Tierra del Fuego in the south. This stretch accounts for nearly 15 percent of the Earth's total land surface area, also serving as host to over half a billion inhabitants, an immense wealth of valuable exports, and a booming tourism industry that draws over 70 million annual visitors. In general the term "Latin America" is applicable to any of the Romance language–speaking countries of the American continents, although in practice it is predominantly used to refer only to those countries that were formerly colonies of Portugal and Spain.

The modern identity of this cultural region— both the characteristics shared uniformly by all its inhabitants and the regional and political differences across its nations—would not exist as we know it had it not been for a series of decisive actions at the hands of a group of charismatic, principled, and effective rebel generals in the early 19th century. These leaders, among whom the best known are perhaps Simón Bolívar and José de San Martín, are now canonized as the fathers of Latin American independence.

On September 6, 1815, while in exile in Kingston, Jamaica, Bolívar wrote a letter known simply as the "Jamaica Letter," which would later find its place secured in history. In this document he

SIMÓN BOLÍVAR LED THE LATIN AMERICAN INDEPENDENCE MOVEMENT IN NORTHERN SOUTH AMERICA. HIS "JAMAICA LETTER," WRITTEN IN 1815, ENCOURAGED THE REGION TO ADOPT CENTRALIZED REPUBLICAN GOVERNMENT, WHICH MANY OF THE FORMER COLONIES EVENTUALLY DID.

recounts the history predating the Latin American movements for independence as well as their more direct causes and—perhaps most importantly—possible outcomes. Citing the struggles historically faced by those engaged in fights for independence, Bolívar acknowledges the difficulty of achieving liberation from tyrannical forces. Yet, he is persistent about the goals that he and his fellow revolutionary generals hold: "Despite the convictions of history, South Americans have made efforts to obtain liberal, even perfect, institutions, doubtless out of that instinct to aspire to the greatest possible happiness, which . . . is bound to follow in civil societies founded on the principles of justice, liberty, and equality." The persistence of Bolívar and other key leaders would eventually prove victorious. While at that pivotal moment in Latin American history the future was most definitely uncertain, the current state of colonial affairs was no longer bearable.

Bolívar and San Martín were just two of the important figures that helped push for Latin American independence. Catholic priest Miguel Hidalgo y Costilla is considered the father of independence in Mexico, where to this day the anniversary of his declaration of revolution against Spain is celebrated as Independence Day. Upon his execution in 1811 he was succeeded by José María Morelos, a fellow priest who would go on to help draft the first independent constitution of Mexico.

Bernardo O'Higgins of Chile would also go down in the annals of Latin American history as a father of the revolution. O'Higgins developed much of his nationalistic fervor while living abroad in Spain and London. There he participated in secret meetings with other revolutionaries of Latin America. Upon returning to Chile he would find himself in a long struggle to oust royalist forces loyal to Spain and help declare the Chilean Republic.

These leaders and others came from diverse corners of the Spanish American empire. While they each had different individual plans for their liberation from the Spaniards, their ability to unite, support each other, and cross boundaries in a common struggle was one of the most influential factors in their eventual success.

The quest by these Latin American leaders for governments based on the aforementioned principles—justice, liberty, and equality—came after centuries of monarchic rule, intense economic and political restrictions, and a class system that Bolívar described in his "Jamaica Letter" as feudal for its relegation of the *criollos*, or Spanish Americans born in the Americas, to a societal position lower than the *peninsulares*, Spaniards who had been born in Spain.

The European colonization of the Americas dated back to Christopher Columbus's voyage in 1492. When Columbus stepped foot on the island of Hispaniola (now divided between the Dominican Republic and Haiti), few truly anticipated the vastness of the so-called New World or the extent to which colonization would transform its physical and human landscape. In Columbus's footsteps followed numerous *conquistadores* in search of gold, slaves, and new territories that could form part of the growing European empires—most notably those of the Iberian Peninsula. Unlike other colonial powers that were often satisfied with simply reaping economic benefits from their colonies, Spain had an interest in occupying its new territories, bringing its culture, language, and—most notably—its Roman Catholic religion with it. Thus began a 300-year period during which the American continents were to be the subjects of a distant authority invested in self-seeking interests.

Societal problems in the colonial Americas were numerous. European-introduced diseases made mortality rates spike among large portions of the indigenous populations.

From the 1500s to the 1800s between 10 and 15 million African slaves were taken to Latin America (mostly Brazil and the Caribbean)—more than 20 times the number sold to the English colonies that became the United States. Over time a class system developed in the Americas that privileged those with "purer" blood and closer ties to the Iberian homeland.

The *peninsulares* ("peninsulars") ranked highest. They were any of the colonial residents of Latin America who had been born in Spain. They enjoyed special favour of the Spanish crown and were often rewarded with lucrative and honorific colonial posts, both civil and ecclesiastic. Below them were the *criollos* ("Creoles"). Creoles were full-blooded Spaniards who had been born in the Americas. Creoles were generally excluded from high office in both church and state, even though they were legally equal to the Spaniards. Discrimination in Spanish crown policy excluded Creoles from the positions occupied by peninsulars and severely restricted the Creoles' commercial activities.

Below both the peninsulars and Creoles ranked numerous other racial groups including *mestizos* ("mixed persons," or persons of combined indigenous American and European heritage), *mulatos* ("mulattoes," or those of combined African and European descent), *zambos* (those of mixed indigenous and African heritage), Africans, and indigenous Americans. The complex racial mixes that occurred in colonial America led to countless divisions, labels, and hypothetical classes to follow, but the general trend was clear: those with "purer" European heritage and closer ties to Iberia were favored by the crowns. The middle groups, including those in the racially mixed categories, did not have excellent work opportunities or much room for societal advancement.

In addition to gradually growing frustrations with the societal class system, another of the building frustrations for Creoles in the Americas was a system of trade restrictions that economists would later come to denote mercantilism. The term was coined in 1776 by Scottish economist Adam Smith to give name to a practice common in Europe from the 16th to 18th centuries that promoted governmental regulation of a nation's economy for the purpose of augmenting state power at the expense of rival national powers. It was the economic counterpart of political absolutism.

In Latin America mercantilism found its practice in the Spanish *flota* ("fleet") system. Spain acted upon the as-yet-undefined mercantile theory when, in 1565, it perfected a system by which all legal trade with its American colonies was restricted to two annual fleets between Seville and designated ports on the Gulf of Mexico and Caribbean. The outgoing ships bore manufactured articles; returning, their cargo consisted partly of gold and silver bars. The Spanish fleet system continued for nearly two centuries. Creoles were frustrated by the system, which limited their trading and export opportunities exclusively to Spain and shut Latin America out of the global market. By the late 1700s many of the frustrations long held by the Creoles had mounted in response to new reforms in Spain, an increasing perception of Spain as an out-of-touch and distant government, and external events that ushered in a revolutionary spirit.

A series of wars fought in the 17th century had weakened Spain's power in Europe, although it was still the greatest imperial power. Its central problem thus became to maintain what remained of its European possessions and to retain control of its American empire. In the 17th century the greatest threat had come from a land power, France, jealous of

Habsburg power in Europe; in the 18th it was to come from a sea power, England, while the Austrian Habsburgs became the main continental enemy of Spain.

In 1759 Charles III assumed the Spanish throne. With his reign came a series of reforms known as the "Caroline" reforms. The centrepiece of Caroline reforms was the introduction of the intendant system in the colonies to tighten up local administration. Most dramatic of all was the abolition of the monopoly of Cadiz, by which all trade to the colonies had to go through that port. Beginning in 1778 other Spanish ports outside of Castile (the traditional central region of Spain where the throne lay) could trade directly with the colonies. The Caroline reforms boosted trade, but imperial free trade would not satisfy the growing demand from Creole producers for free trade with all nations. Nor did the colonial oligarchs desire efficient government and higher taxation; they preferred bad government that let them control their own affairs.

Developments in Spain did not alone lay the foundations for the Latin American wars of independence. Foreign intellectual influence and a general spirit of global revolution contributed as well. Latin American elites showed familiarity with the Enlightenment ideals espoused by such thinkers as Thomas Hobbes, John Locke, Montesquieu, and Jean-Jacques Rousseau. The French Revolution and Napoleon's leadership in France also contributed to a general revolutionary spirit. When an alliance formed between France and Spain, Charles IV granted Napoleon entry through Spain to conquer Portugal. The flight of the Portuguese monarchy to its Brazilian colony would be the first step toward the latter's eventual independence.

In 1776, 13 of the British colonies in North America declared independence, soon becoming the United States of

America. In 1791 a massive slave revolt in the French Caribbean colony of Saint-Domingue sparked a general insurrection against the plantation system and French colonial power. By the first years of the 19th century, the independent nation of Haiti emerged from that struggle. The revolutionary spirit was ripe, and while Latin American Creoles feared a complete overturning of the power structures that kept them in a relatively high social position (such as that which had occurred in the Haitian Revolution), developments in Europe and the Americas seemed to imply that the time was ripe.

Once the spark was set off, independence for Latin America swept across the colonies rather swiftly. Between 1808 and 1826—a mere 18 years—all of Latin America, with the exception of the Spanish colonies of Cuba and Puerto Rico, freed itself from the rule of the two European powers that had politically dominated the region since the first days of exploration and conquest. The earliest years of revolution were difficult. Independence in the north came at the hands of Bolívar in Venezuela. From the south it was guided by San Martín in Argentina. Each fought in his respective region, facing fierce loyalist forces and persistent efforts at the hands of the Spanish throne. By the second decade of the 19th century Spain had largely put the revolutions in check. It was at that moment that Bolívar found himself in exile writing the "Jamaica Letter" and expressing his undying faith in a government founded on justice, liberty, and equality.

The persistence of these leaders would pay off. Each attempt by the Spaniards and loyalists to squash the revolutions was met by a renewed effort that, just 11 years after the composition of the "Jamaica Letter," would find its victory. Bolívar swept down from the north and San Martín up from the south, each aided by regional leaders and determined to liberate not just their own colonies but all of Latin America from Spanish tyranny. They met on the central Pacific coast and, in 1826, stamped out the last of the loyalist resistance.

Hindsight always provides a clearer vision around the causes and consequences of historical events. Thus today the steady development of tensions in the Latin American colonies over a 300-year period and the triggers that ignited said fuel could not be clearer. Undesirable economic restrictions and consistent subjugation of most of the population to a lower social status made the conditions for revolution in the Americas ripe. With opportune external developments and swift-acting, insightful leaders, Latin American independence was all but guaranteed. An understanding of the historical causes, leading figures, quintessential episodes, and struggles that followed Latin American independence are invaluable for any understanding of the culture, politics, and social identity of the region today.

# LATIN AMERICA UNDER COLONIZATION

A series of important changes occurring in Spanish America in the 18th century is often associated with dynastic changes in Spain—the replacement of the Habsburgs, who had ruled Spain since the early 16th century, by a branch of the French Bourbons in 1700. Little altered in the Spanish territories until more than 50 years later, however, especially during the reign of Charles III (1759–88). Internal evolution and worldwide developments were doubtless more important in bringing about independence movements than the policy of a particular dynasty or ruler.

## ECONOMY AND SOCIETY

Demographic growth picked up sharply after about the mid-18th century in all areas about which information is available and in all sectors of the population. At the same time, economic activity increased in bulk, and prices rose steadily instead of fluctuating as they had been doing for centuries. Silver production, which was still at the base of the export economy of the old central areas, increased sharply, especially in Mexico, and so did the scale of operations and the input of capital, with strong participation by merchant-financiers. At the same time, local textile production had grown in size and economic importance, as demand rose in its market—humble Hispanized people in the city and countryside.

The large merchants had continued the process of localization to the point where only their birth was foreign; large firms tended to pass from a Spanish immigrant owner to his immigrant nephew. In every other way—marriage, investment, and residence pattern—the merchants were part of the local milieu, and, since export-import commerce was so important to the economy, they had risen to the top on the local scene. The wealthiest of them owned strings of haciendas in addition to their commercial and mining interests, and they acquired titles of high nobility.

Racial and cultural fusion had advanced so far that the categorization embodied in the ethnic hierarchy could no longer capture it. Labels proliferated to designate complex mixtures, but the new terms sat lightly on those so labeled and often had no legal status. In everyday life, people who were able to function within a Hispanic context were often not labeled at all; many others changed almost at will from one category to another. One reaction to the excessive categorization was simplification, with only three categories—Spaniards, *castas* (people of mixed race), and Indians—and often only two—Indians and others. The people of mixed descent were now so fully acculturated and so deeply embedded in local Hispanic society that they were qualified for and began to compete for nearly all positions except the very highest. There was, naturally, a reaction on the part of those most highly placed. As mulattoes entered the universities, ordinances began to declare that they were not eligible. With the children of wealthy Spaniards, humbler and racially mixed Spaniards, and *castas* all intermarrying widely, government and the church began to resist, declaring marriages between those differently labeled to be illegal and reinforcing the authority of parents in disallowing matches.

## CREOLES AND PENINSULARS

"Creole" (in Spanish, *criollo*) referred originally to any person of European (mostly French or Spanish) or African descent born in the West Indies or parts of French or Spanish America (and thus naturalized in those regions rather than in the parents' home country). "Peninsular" referred to any of the colonial residents of Latin America from the 16th through the early 19th centuries who had been born in Spain. The name refers to the Iberian Peninsula, which is made up of Spain and Portugal.

Although legally Spaniards and Creoles were equal, discrimination arose from Spanish crown policy aimed at rewarding its favoured Spanish subjects with lucrative and honorific colonial posts, while excluding Creoles from such positions and severely restricting their commercial activities. Thus, there was enmity between the two groups. Creoles had contemptuous names for peninsulars: *gachupines* ("those with spurs") in Mexico and *chapetones* ("tenderfeet") in South America. Peninsulars enjoyed the special favour of the Spanish crown and were appointed to most of the leading civil and ecclesiastical posts under the colonial regime.

(*continued on the next page*)

**3**

## CREOLES AND PENINSULARS
(CONTINUED)

As a result, the Creoles were relegated to second-class status, though they, in turn, enjoyed many advantages over Indians, blacks, and those of mixed blood (mestizos). The Creoles acquired a reputation for being superficial and indolent, but these generalizations were made without the necessary acknowledgement that Creole education, practical experience, and, especially, economic and political opportunities were quite limited. The Creoles led the revolutions that expelled the colonial regime from Spanish America in the early 19th century. After independence in Mexico, Peru, and elsewhere, Creoles entered the ruling class. They were generally conservative and cooperated with the higher clergy, the army, large landowners, and, later, foreign investors. Meanwhile, the peninsulars were, in many cases, driven out.

Such reactions did little to change the basic reality: the intermediate groups had grown and were continuing to grow to the extent that they could no longer be confined to their traditional intermediary functions. There were too many of them for all to become majordomos (stewards) and artisans, and, in any case, many people called Indians by now could speak Spanish and handle tasks for which intermediaries had previously been required. Since the people in the middle were no longer at a premium, their remuneration often decreased. If some pressed on into the higher strata, others were reduced to positions traditionally belonging to Indians, such as permanent labourer. In many areas the mixed groups were pouring into indigenous settlements at such a rate as to disrupt them and change their character.

## VICEROYALTY OF NEW SPAIN

The Viceroyalty of New Spain was the first of the four viceroyalties that Spain created to govern its conquered lands in the New World. Established in 1535, it initially included all land north of the Isthmus of Panama under Spanish control. This later came to include upper and lower California, the area that is now the central and southwestern portion of the United States, and territory eastward along the Gulf of Mexico to Florida. The Viceroyalty of New Spain was also charged with governing Spain's Caribbean possessions. Later, in 1565, the newly conquered Philippines were placed under the jurisdiction of New Spain.

Although technically superior in governing authority, the viceroy in New Spain was hampered in practice from exerting that authority by the considerable independence of governors and royal *audiencias* (high courts) in many of the subordinate

By the eighteenth century, Spain had organized its vast American colonies into four viceroyalties. Portugal controlled Brazil, and France maintained the small colony of Guiana. The Spaniards never successfully settled the semiarid plateau of Patagonia.

areas. His power was largely confined to central and southern Mexico—from San Luis Potosí in the north to the Isthmus of Tehuantepec in the south. Within this territory, the viceroys of New Spain aided in converting the native population to Christianity, developed an array of educational institutions, and oversaw an economy based almost entirely on mining and ranching. During the first 100 years of Spanish rule, the Indian population of New Spain declined from an estimated 25 million to 1 million as a result of maltreatment, disease, and disruption of their cultures.

The first viceroy in New Spain was Antonio de Mendoza, who ruled from 1535 to 1549, then served as viceroy of Peru, where he died after one year in office. In New Spain, he dispatched Francisco Coronado on his expedition northward while ameliorating some of the worst abuses of the *conquistadores*. He supported the church in its work with the native population.

After a period of decline in the late 17th and early 18th centuries, the Viceroyalty of New Spain took on new life when refreshed by two distinguished men: Antonio María de Bucareli (1771–79) and Juan Vicente de Güemes Pacheco de Padilla, the second count of Revillagigedo (1789–94); the latter was the last able viceroy in New Spain.

In the 18th century, more Spanish women immigrated to New Spain, accompanying their fathers and brothers, and greatly altered the social composition of colonial society. Spanish women, especially those who could bring a respectable dowry to marriage, were greatly sought. Although Spanish society, like other European societies, was patriarchal in its relegation of women, wives and daughters could inherit property. By the late colonial period several women could be found running businesses in the cities or administering rural property in New Spain.

A fundamental shift in the governance of New Spain occurred as a result of the War of the Spanish Succession

(1701–14), when the house of Bourbon replaced the Habsburgs on the Spanish throne. The Bourbon kings were enlightened despots whose major interests lay in increasing economic returns, and they introduced many French practices and ideas into the overseas administration of the Spanish empire.

Among the notable administrative reforms undertaken by Charles III in 1784 was the creation of 18 intendancies within which local governments were also reorganized. Headed by the intendancy of Mexico, each intendancy (*intendencia*) was presided over by an intendente who was given considerable autonomy in increasing economic production within his sphere, developing useful arts and sciences, and bettering education and social conditions, all of the latter less for altruistic than for economic reasons.

# VICEROYALTY OF PERU

The Viceroyalty of Peru was the second of the four viceroyalties that Spain created to govern its domains in the Americas. Established in 1543, the viceroyalty initially included all of South America under Spanish control except for the coast of what is now Venezuela. Until nearly the end of the colonial era, Peru was considered the most valuable Spanish possession in the Americas. It produced vast quantities of silver bullion for shipment to Europe, especially from the mines at Potosí. Thriving on the enforced labour of Indians, an exploitative society of mine operators and merchant princes lived in splendour in the coastal city of Lima. Access to easy wealth, however, was one of the major contributing factors to political instability in the region. Geography was another; Lima's position along the western coast of South America limited effective

**7**

Engraved for BANKES's New System of GEOGRAPHY Published by Royal Authority.

View of POTOSI in the Kingdom of Peru in South America.

**SILVER DEPOSITS WERE FIRST DISCOVERED IN THE POTOSÍ REGION IN 1545. WORKING IN THE MINES WAS SO DANGEROUS THAT EIGHT MILLION INDIAN AND AFRICAN SLAVES DIED THERE BY 1825.**

communication with Spain, and the rigours of the terrain (the Andes Mountains) made Peru very difficult to govern.

During the later 17th century, Peru experienced difficulties. Some of these, such as increasing contraband trade with non-Spanish merchants, attacks by pirates, and the growth of corruption among government officials, reflected the internal decay of Spain and the decline of its international power. Contributing to Peruvian difficulties was the decline of its production of precious metals.

A series of governmental reforms complicated Peru's problems in the 18th century. The first to seriously affect Peru was the establishment of the new Viceroyalty of New Granada, ending Peru's control over northern South America and resulting in its loss to New Granada of the thriving port of Guayaquil (now in Ecuador). For the next few decades, reforms by the Bourbon rulers of Spain, together with overall expansion of the economy, improved conditions in Peru. In 1777–78, however, the Spanish government established another viceroyalty, that of Río de la Plata, this time depriving the Peruvian viceroy of authority over Upper Peru and the areas of present-day Argentina, Paraguay, and Uruguay. Chile, which had always been a poor colony because it had only very limited precious metal, was reconstituted as a virtually autonomous captaincy general. Following the disastrous loss of the silver mines of Upper Peru, the Viceroyalty of Peru was still more weakened by reforms in the trade system, which permitted merchants in ports on the Atlantic and the Pacific to trade directly with Spain.

# VICEROYALTY OF NEW GRANADA

With its Caribbean coast, Venezuela had long been in a relatively favourable position in regard to potential availability of markets. By the 17th century the Caracas region was exporting cacao to Mexico, where most of the market for that product was then located, enabling it to begin buying African slaves for labour. As Europe joined the market and absorbed larger quantities of cacao by the late 18th century, Caracas became an urban centre comparable in size and institutionalization to Buenos Aires (though without a viceroy), and it had a better-developed hinterland of secondary settlements. The population along the coast was mainly European, African, and mixtures thereof.

The Viceroyalty of New Granada, which included present-day Colombia, Panama (after 1751), Venezuela, and Ecuador, was created in 1717–23 and reconstituted in 1740, opening a new era. In the next decades the crown introduced political and economic measures to reorganize and strengthen the empire by greater centralization of authority, improved administration and communication, and freer development and movement of trade within the empire. Population grew, trade increased, and prosperity touched the colonial subjects. There was a spurt of intellectual activity and the formation of a corps of intellectuals and professional men among Creoles, many in government positions. The small Creole officer corps came into being when Charles III, then king of Spain, authorized militia defense units in the colonies. A relatively large group of wealthy landowners and merchants constituted the economic community that supported these new groups. In 1781 peasants and artisans at Socorro originated the Comunero Rebellion in response to tax increases; although some Creoles helped lead the rebels to Bogotá, most hesitated to support the uprising or even helped to undermine it. Between 1785 and 1810 in New Granada the outlook of the Creole upper and middle groups changed from resistance against political and economic change to a quest for specific changes in imperial policies. In 1809 they moved toward the free enterprise system, the abolition of slavery, restrictions on government, and worldwide freedom of trade.

Educational reforms played an important role in the changing outlook of the Granadine Creoles. Archbishop Caballero y Góngora as viceroy (1782–88) made education one of his main interests. He modernized the program of studies in the schools, opened a school of mines, and initiated the botanical expedition under the able guidance of naturalist José Celestino Mutis. The new institute trained many of the major figures of the independence movement. The first newspaper and theatre were introduced during the 1790s. A new interest in writing developed, and intellectual gatherings for discussion were introduced. In 1808 the allegiance of the Granadines to the crown remained unquestioned except for a few individuals. The once warm loyalty of the Creole middle and upper classes, however, was cooling under the pressure of economic interests, scandals in the royal family, and persistent social tension between Creole and European Spaniards.

# VICEROYALTY OF THE RÍO DE LA PLATA

Well into the 18th century, the perception that Mexico and Peru formed the centre and all the rest the periphery was still valid. By the last decades of the century, however, things were moving quickly in a different direction, favouring the Atlantic seaboard. European demand for tropical crops and even for temperate products, especially hides, increased substantially. At the same time, ships grew larger and faster. As a result, transatlantic ship-ment of bulk products became more viable, and trade routes shifted.

The decision to create a fourth viceroyalty, the Viceroy-alty of the Río de la Plata, was a result both of King Charles III's desire to decentralize the rule of his Spanish-American empire and of a recognition that the area south of Brazil required greater military defenses in view of Portuguese encroach-ments along the northern shore of the Río de la Plata. Spain also wanted to curtail contraband trade between Portuguese Brazil and Buenos Aires. In addition, by the 1760s the British had made clear their intention to take the Falkland (Malvinas) Islands. Although Spain pressured the British out of temporary possession of the islands, the need for greater military control of the South Atlantic region had become apparent.

## ARGENTINA

The Río de La Plata region had been very much on the edges of the Latin American world since the conquest. The first founding of Buenos Aires in the early 16th century had failed, the survivors having taken refuge in the lands of the semisedentary Guaraní of Paraguay. The most developed area was the northwest interior, closest to the Potosí mining region, which supplied the mines with various products.

Buenos Aires was eventually refounded but remained a tiny, struggling port. The plains were inhabited by wild cattle (descendants of domestic animals introduced into the region earlier), nonsedentary Indians, and some highly localized mestizos later to be called gauchos.

Starting in the 1770s, improved transatlantic navigation, combined with liberalization of the imperial trading system, transformed the region. Buenos Aires began to be able to compete with the older route through Panama and Peru in importing European goods for the mining region and exporting silver. The immigration of merchants and others increased. Taking advantage of the opportunity, the crown created the Viceroyalty of the Río de la Plata based in Buenos Aires (1776), including the Potosí mining region, which was taken from

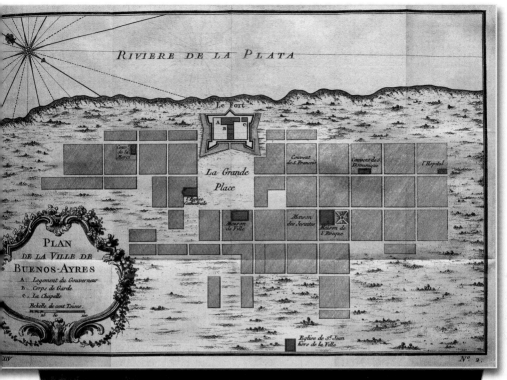

*SOON AFTER THIS MAP OF BUENOS AIRES WAS PRODUCED IN 1763, THE CITY WAS OPENED TO TRANSATLANTIC TRADE AND GREW IN POPULATION AND IMPORTANCE TO THE SPANISH EMPIRE.*

Peru. By carving the new viceroyalty from lands formerly part of the Viceroyalty of Peru, Spain intended to put its east-coast dominions in a better defensive position. The chief threat came from Brazil, which was growing rapidly in population, wealth, and military potential. For the first time, the port of Buenos Aires was opened to transatlantic trade with Spain and, through Spain, with other countries. This resulted in a great increase in both legal trade and smuggling. Buenos Aires became a capital with all the institutions associated with Lima or Mexico City. The city's population, including a substantial number of Africans because of its location on a slave route and its new wealth, grew explosively, and it began to exercise dominance over the interior, reversing the older scheme. Intellectually, interest in the new ideas of the European Enlightenment found fertile soil in cosmopolitan Buenos Aires.

Yet Buenos Aires was not quite like Lima or Mexico City; it showed its newness and was in some ways tangential. The merchants of Buenos Aires had the same Spanish origins as their counterparts in Mexico City, but they were more closely tied to Spain, much like central-area merchants in the conquest period. They were more dominant locally, for there were no long-established families to compete with, and they came close to monopolizing the capital's municipal council. But they were far less wealthy than the largest Mexico City merchants, established no noble titles, and owned few or no rural estates. Indeed, there were no estates to buy: haciendas existed in the older northwestern region, but on the plains or pampas around Buenos Aires estate development had hardly begun. The hide export industry that now began to become prominent rested at first mainly on hunting wild animals; the merchants who exported hides were still secondary to those importing merchandise and exporting silver. Only in the last years before independence did merchants and others finally begin to build up estates and raise cattle in the more customary manner.

## PARAGUAY

Paraguay remained in relative isolation and poverty, participating in the money economy by sending its yerba maté (a tealike beverage) toward Peru. For more than 150 years from early in the 17th century, Jesuit communal missions in the

Paraná and Uruguay basins of southeastern Paraguay governed the lives of 150,000 Indians in 30 *reducciones*, or settlements. These were centres of religious conversion, agricultural and pastoral production, and manufacturing and trade; they served also as strategic outposts against Portuguese expansion from southern Brazil. Isolated from the heart of Paraguay, which centred on Asunción, the missions became an autonomous military, political, and economic "state within a state," increasingly exciting the envy of the Spanish landowners in the Asunción area. In the period 1721–35 the latter waged a struggle to overthrow the Jesuit monopoly of Indian trade and labour. Unaided, the settlements also had to defend themselves against slave raiders from São Paulo and, in 1754–57, a combined Spanish-Portuguese attack that was designed to enforce a territorial partition of the mission settlements. Defiance of such powerful groups paved the way for the expulsion of the Jesuits in 1767. The settlements were abandoned, the Indians were absorbed by either the landed estates or the jungle, the settlements fell into ruin, and economic activity ceased.

In 1776 the new Viceroyalty of the Río de la Plata effectively made Asunción and all of Paraguay dependent on Buenos Aires, thus ending the region's colonial dominance.

## URUGUAY

In 1776 the Banda Oriental became part of the Viceroyalty of the Río de la Plata; however, Montevideo was still allowed to send shipments directly to Spain rather than clearing them first at Buenos Aires. Montevideo became the major Spanish port of the South Atlantic, and the process of dividing the Banda Oriental into huge unfenced ranches began.

By 1800 there were approximately 10,000 people in Montevideo and another 20,000 elsewhere in Uruguay. About one-third of the total were African slaves, most of whom worked on *estancias* (ranches), in *saladeros* (meat-salting operations), and in households. Uruguay's small but growing middle class included petty merchants, artisans, and military officers of mestizo and European ancestry. At the apex of society were wealthy traders, bankers, *estancieros* (ranch owners), and high-ranking government officials. Most of the elite originated from—or principally resided in—Catalonia, the Basque Country, the Canary Islands, and other Spanish European lands. Few Indian groups survived into the 19th century; the last large-scale massacre of Indian peoples occurred at Salsipuedes in 1831, and by mid century scant vestiges of indigenous culture remained.

# CAUSES OF REVOLUTION

After three centuries of colonial rule, independence came rather suddenly to most of Spanish and Portuguese America. Between 1808 and 1826 all of Latin America except the Spanish colonies of Cuba and Puerto Rico slipped out of the hands of the Iberian powers that had ruled the region since the conquest. The rapidity and timing of that dramatic change were the result of a combination of long-building tensions in colonial rule and a series of external events.

Although many wars in the 17th century had weakened Spain's power in Europe, the country still remained the world's greatest imperial power. Spain's central problem in the 17th century had been to maintain what remained of its European possessions and to retain control of its American empire. At

*IN THE 1704 BATTLE OF BLENHEIM DURING THE WAR OF THE SPANISH SUCCESSION, THE ENGLISH DUKE OF MARLBOROUGH AND PRINCE EUGENE OF SAVOY, WHO SERVED THE AUSTRIAN HOLY EMPEROR, WERE VICTORIOUS.*

the beginning of the 18th century, both tasks appeared to be beyond the military and economic resources of the monarchy.

In 1700 (by the will of the childless Charles II) the duc d'Anjou, grandson of Louis XIV of France, became Philip V of Spain, thus replacing the Habsburg dynasty with the Bourbons. Both England and Austria opposed Philip because they did not want the Bourbons to gain more power, which led to the War of the Spanish Succession (1701–14). In the end, Philip V remained king of Spain, but the war cost Spain many of its possessions outside Iberia. The treaties of Maastricht and Utrecht (1713) stripped it of its European possessions (Belgium, Luxembourg, Milan, Sardinia, Sicily, and Naples) and gave Britain Gibraltar and Minorca and the right to send one ship a year to trade with Spanish America. The Bourbon dynasty then undertook a program of reform during the 18th century, seeking to promote the economic development of their colonies, improve colonial defenses, and provide more efficient government.

# THE BOURBON REFORMS

The Enlightenment, emanating to a large extent from France, penetrated both Spain (aided by the French origin of the Bourbons) and Spanish America in the 18th century. By the late part of the century individuals and organized societies in many of the American territories were producing journals and books in the manner of the work of the French Encyclopédistes, promoting reason, universality, science, modernity, and efficiency. Most Spanish-American writers, while staying in close touch with European currents, were concerned with the development, in practical terms, of their own regions.

Enlightenment philosophy bore importantly on government, which was called on to be more rationally unified, efficient, and free of church influence. Such ideas affected policy makers for the Spanish crown, and a series of activist royal measures of the 18th century were carried out in that spirit. Yet the timing and the nature of these moves had at least as much to do with changing conditions as with ideology. Most reforms came in a bundle in the late 18th century, the creation in 1739 of the Viceroyalty of New Granada based in Santa Fé (Bogotá) being an exception.

## POLITICAL REFORMS

A major Bourbon reform, taking place mainly in the 1780s, was the creation of large districts called intendancies (the word and model were French). Each was headed by an official with extensive powers called an intendant, who was directly responsible to the crown in Spain. The measure was meaningful because royal government in the provinces, outside the seats of the viceroy (the province ruler) and the captains general, had hardly existed. It was as though a host of provincial cities received their own viceroy. One result, and indeed the one most intended, was an increase in revenue collection; another, not intended, was decentralization and bickering. The intendancy seats were not arbitrarily created or chosen but were mainly large cities that were still bishoprics, or long-lasting, large-scale mining centres. The change was realistic in that it recognized the immense growth and consolidation of provincial Hispanic centres that had occurred in the centuries since the first establishment of the viceroyalties, and for that reason it took hold. Less successful was the attempt to introduce similar officials at a lower level in the Indian countryside.

## MILITARY REFORMS

Military affairs were a second target of reform. Spanish America had long been defended by a patchwork of viceregal guards, port garrisons, half-fictional militias, and some forts and paid soldiers on frontiers with hostile Indians, but it had not had a formal military organization. In the late 18th century it acquired one, partly because of an increased foreign threat (Havana was occupied by the

British in 1762–63), partly because the Bourbons imagined the army to be the most responsive branch available to them, and partly because professionalization of the military was an international trend of the time. A relatively small number of regular units formed the backbone for a larger, more rigorously organized militia. At first the regulars were brought in from Spain, but before long the lower ranks were mainly locals, and locals found entry even into the officer ranks, though the top commanders were usually Spanish born. The military was primarily Hispanic, with Indians taking part only under exceptional circumstances, and it reflected local society, with officers drawn from prominent families and many persons of mixed descent and Africans among the enlisted men. Organized in local districts, the units' loyalties were above all local as well.

## RELIGIOUS REFORMS

Government in Bourbon times was not antireligious, but it was sufficiently affected by the spirit of the times to be quite anticlerical. The most decisive of the measures taken was the expulsion of the Jesuit order from Spanish America and Spain in 1767. Preceded by similar actions in Portugal and France, the move was part of an international wave, but it also made excellent sense in purely Spanish-American terms. Although the Jesuits were the wealthiest of the orders, they had arrived last, had fierce rivals in other branches of the church, and counted few locals among their members. Thus their expulsion was greeted with (usually hidden) approval by many. The crown in general tried to further the secular clergy over the religious orders (imagined to be more independent-minded), but the policy had little effect except in areas where the secular clergy, which grew with the expansion of civil society, was already on the rise. Almost on the eve of independence, the crown attempted to confiscate church property, but the measure proved hard to enforce.

## ECONOMIC REFORMS

The late Bourbons favoured more active encouragement of the economy and even intervention in it. They provided tax reductions and technical aid for the silver mining industry; they expanded state monopolies beyond the mercury needed for mining to some other commodities, of which tobacco was the most successful. Their largest reform, however, went in the opposite direction, consisting in the declaration of free trade within the Spanish empire, so that any port could trade with any other at will.

In earlier times the bulk of transatlantic trade had been directed at Mexico and Peru, and annual convoys sponsored by the Spanish government were an efficient way not only to organize the traffic but also to protect it from pirates, who were the main threat. By the 18th century the northern European powers had naval superiority and could easily have destroyed any convoy. Moreover, in Spanish America new central areas had arisen, with a consequent diversification of destinations, and in Spain the north had revived at the expense of the south, where Sevilla and Cádiz had monopolized Indies navigation. Under these changed circumstances, the best arrangement was to allow individual ships to travel between any Spanish port and any American port. The fleet system gradually fell

*A Representation of the SUGAR-CANE and the Art of Making Sugar.*

*Engraved for the Universal Magazine according to Act of Parliament 1749 for J. Hinton at y.e King's Arms in S.t Paul's Church Yard London*

*THIS ENGRAVING ILLUSTRATING THE SUGAR CANE PRODUCTION PROCESS WAS PUBLISHED IN A MAGAZINE IN 1749.*

apart in the 18th century. Imperial free trade was introduced between 1765 and 1789, first affecting Cuba and spreading to all Spanish possessions. The measure coincided with a marked increase in commercial volume; to what extent free trade caused the increase, as opposed to demographic growth in the Indies and industrial growth in Europe, is not clear. Nor are the effects entirely clear. The deluge of goods made it harder for the largest American merchants to be as dominant as previously, and for the first time local textile producers had real competition for the lower end of the market. Even so, the large firms of Mexico City were not destroyed, and the Puebla textile industry continued to grow.

# SOCIAL TENSIONS

The position of the locally born Spaniards, often called Creoles or *criollos* (though they were slow to call themselves that), had been growing stronger all across the postconquest centuries. From an early time they owned most of the rural estates and dominated most of the *cabildos*, or municipal councils. By the 17th century they were a large majority among the secular clergy and prominent in the orders, and as time went on they received more and more of the bishoprics. In the course of the 17th century they achieved appointments as *audiencia* judges in various centres, and by the second half of the 18th century they were dominating, sometimes virtually monopolizing, the membership of *audiencias* all over Spanish America. As the military came into existence, they found prominent places in it. Large mining producers might be either born locally or Spanish-born. Large merchants remained predominantly born in Spain, but they married into local families, whose interests they often served. Each major local Spanish family had members placed strategically across the whole system, creating a strong informal network. Only the viceroys and usually the archbishops were normally recruited from the outside, and even they had local entourages.

As the Bourbon government in Spain became more active late in the 18th century, it wanted a larger place for its own Spanish-born associates and began to view the extent of local American dominance with alarm. The *audiencias* were gradually filled predominantly with Spanish-born judges; nearly all the intendants were outsiders and so were the highest military officers. Yet the basic situation hardly changed, for the Spanish-born appointees had to function in a local milieu, into which they were rapidly absorbed. As independence approached, the local Spaniards or Creoles had influence and experience at all levels of society, economy, and government, but they had been under challenge for a generation or more and were correspondingly resentful.

Consciousness of separateness of various kinds had been growing for a long time. In Mexico, starting as early as the mid-17th century, the illustrious indigenous past and the cult of the Virgin of Guadalupe had become a basis for national pride, promoted above all by Creole priests and scholars. Other areas had approximate equivalents, if not as well-defined. Awareness of ethnic distinctions within the Spanish category increased in the 18th century along with the proliferation of ethnic terminology in general. The Creoles were still mainly called Spaniards, but the new arrivals from Spain, now a small minority, were distinguished from the rest as peninsular or European Spaniards, and in Mexico they received the insulting nickname *gachupín*.

The middle groups, whether humble Spaniards or people in the racially mixed categories, had much reason for discontent. The expansion of the middle left a large segment of the population without employment corresponding to its expectations and capacities. Corporately organized indigenous groups, however, though not in an admirable state economically or in many other respects, were generally little concerned about conditions at a countrywide level. It is not that they were apathetic; all through the intervening centuries they had stood up for themselves, through litigation and sometimes through disturbances and revolts, but they had done so as individual communities. On the nonsedentary fringe, wars and rebellions continued, but this was not different from earlier times. The most volatile element were Spanish-speaking Indians in and around Hispanic communities, who had mobility and broad awareness and whose profile no longer corresponded to the implications and duties of the label "Indian."

# EARLY REBELLIONS

Two large manifestations of the late 18th century can be seen as foreshadowing independence, though it is possible that they did as much to impede it. In 1780–81 the Andean highlands experienced the Túpac Amaru II revolt, which wrested control of much of the region from the ordinary authorities for many months until it was forcibly put down. Túpac Amaru II was a cacique (hereditary chief) in the Tinta region of southern Peru and a descendant of the last Inca ruler, Túpac Amaru. He received a formal Jesuit education but maintained his identification with the Indian population. In 1780 he arrested and executed the *corregidor* (provincial administrator), Antonio Arriaga, on charges of cruelty. This act led to the last general Indian rebellion against Spain, at first with the support of some Creoles (Spaniards born in America). The revolt, which spread throughout southern Peru and into Bolivia and Argentina, lost this support, however, when it became a violent battle between Indians and Europeans. Túpac Amaru II and his family were captured in March 1781 and taken to Cuzco. After being forced to witness the execution of his wife and sons, he was mutilated, drawn and quartered, and beheaded. The revolution continued until the Spanish government issued a general pardon of the insurgents.

The Comunero Rebellion in Colombia began in 1780 in the provincial town of Socorro, a tobacco and textile-producing centre. In response to new tobacco and polling taxes imposed by the Spanish government, insurgents led by Manuela Beltrán in Socorro, Colombia, sparked a revolt that soon spread to neighbouring towns north of Bogotá. The rebels, in addition to demanding the cancellation of taxes, urged such wide-ranging reforms as protection of Indian lands and an increase in the number of Creoles appointed to administrative posts. A combined force of peasants and artisans, with some Creole leaders, marched on Bogotá to deliver the list of demands, which were swiftly met on June 4, 1781. Soon after the main rebel force had dispersed and returned homeward, however, the Spanish viceroy declared the concessions invalid and, reinforced by troops from the coast, moved to quash the vestiges of antigovernment sentiment. Many of the Creoles who had taken part in the uprising had done so reluctantly, and several of them turned informant as the Spanish reasserted control, took prisoners, and executed some rebel leaders. Roman Catholic clergy even threatened divine retribution on peasants harbouring rebellious sympathies. The mestizo peasant leader José Antonio Galán, who attempted to organize a second march on the capital, was hanged on Jan. 30, 1782. Notably, the Comunero rebels had merely sought reforms, not independence, and had marched under the slogan "Long live the king, and down with bad government!" ("¡Viva el rey y muera el mal gobierno!").

Both movements were in immediate response to Bourbon fiscal measures, and both proclaimed ultimate loyalty to the Spanish crown. In Peru especially, there was a strong reaction afterward against both dissent and the indigenous population. The impetus for independence in Spanish South America would eventually come from the newly thriving Atlantic seaboard regions—the former fringes, Venezuela and Argentina—which had mobile Hispanized populations and lacked large groups of sedentary Indians. In Mexico too, things would start in the very similar near north of the country.

In Brazil, the local Portuguese population had a position quite comparable to that of the Spanish-American Creoles, but it was not so far advanced, and the situation had not become polarized. Transatlantic mobility still made itself felt,

# THE HAITIAN REVOLUTION

Beginning in 1791, a massive slave revolt on the island of Hispaniola sparked a general insurrection against the plantation system and French colonial power. The rebellion developed into both a civil war, pitting blacks and mulattoes against whites, and an international conflict, as England and Spain supported the white plantation owners and rebels, respectively. By the first years of the 19th century, the rebels had shattered what had been a model colony and forged the independent nation of Haiti.

The revolution was actually a series of conflicts during the period 1791–1804 that involved shifting alliances of Haitian slaves, *affranchis* (free mulattoes or blacks), mulattoes, and colonists, as well as British and French army troops. Several factors precipitated the event, including the affranchis' frustrations with a racist society, the French Revolution, nationalistic rhetoric expressed during Vodou ceremonies, the continuing brutality of slave owners, and wars between European powers.

Vincent Ogé, a mulatto who had lobbied the Parisian assembly for colonial reforms, led an uprising in late 1790 but was captured, tortured, and executed. In May 1791 the French revolutionary government granted citizenship to the wealthier affranchis, but Haiti's European population refused to comply with the law. Within two months isolated fighting broke out between Europeans and affranchis, and in August thousands of slaves rose in rebellion. The Europeans attempted to appease the mulattoes in order to quell the slave revolt, and the French assembly granted citizenship to all affranchis in April 1792. The country was torn by rival factions, some of which were supported by Spanish colonists in Santo Domingo (on the eastern side of the island, which later became the Dominican Republic) or by British troops from Jamaica. In 1793 Léger Félicité Sonthonax, who was sent from France to maintain order, offered freedom to slaves who joined his army; he soon abolished slavery altogether, and the following year the French government confirmed his decision. Spain ceded the rest of the island to France in the Treaty of Basel (1795), but war in Europe precluded the actual transfer of possession.

In the late 1790s Toussaint Louverture, a military leader and former slave, gained control of several areas and earned the initial support of French agents. He gave nominal allegiance to France while pursuing his own political and military designs, which included negotiating with the British, and in May 1801 he had himself named "governor-general for life." Napoléon Bonaparte (later Napoleon I), wishing to maintain control of the island, attempted to restore the old regime (and European rule) by sending his brother-in-law, General Charles Leclerc, with an experienced force from Saint-Domingue that included several exiled mulatto officers. Toussaint struggled for several months against Leclerc's forces before agreeing to an armistice in May 1802; however, the French broke the agreement and imprisoned him in France. He died on April 7, 1803.

Jean-Jacques Dessalines and Henry Christophe led a black army against the French in 1802, following evidence that Napoleon intended to restore slavery in Saint-Domingue as he had done in other French possessions. They defeated the French commander

(continued on the next page)

# THE HAITIAN REVOLUTION (CONTINUED)

and a large part of his army, and in November 1803 the viscount de Rochambeau surrendered the remnant of the expedition. The French withdrew from Haiti but maintained a presence in the eastern part of the island until 1809. On Jan. 1, 1804, the entire island was declared independent under the Arawak-derived name of Haiti. Many European powers and their Caribbean surrogates ostracized Haiti, fearing the spread of slave revolts.

with many leading Brazilian Portuguese having been educated in Portugal. Locally born Portuguese had long participated in the Brazilian high court system, but they had never been a majority as in Spanish America. Two well-known rebellious incidents occurring in the 1780s and '90s, in Minas Gerais and Bahia, did not have full support even locally.

Latin America approached independence after a thoroughgoing ethnic and cultural transformation across a period of over three centuries. That process did not destroy the indigenous component, which was still very much alive corporately and culturally in the old central areas and some other regions and had also affected and entered into the mixed Iberian societies that had come to dominance. Even where it almost disappeared, the indigenous factor was important, for its weakness or absence was what allowed certain regions to become more European and African. Most of the independent countries that arose in the early 19th century went back to indigenous culture areas that had been re-formed into functional units under Iberian management in the 16th century.

# ENLIGHTENMENT IDEAS

The reforms imposed by the Spanish Bourbons in the 18th century provoked great instability in the relations between the rulers and their colonial subjects in the Americas. Many Creoles felt Bourbon policy to be an unfair attack on their wealth, political power, and social status. Others did not suffer during the second half of the 18th century; indeed, the gradual loosening of trade restrictions actually benefited some Creoles in Venezuela and certain areas that had moved from the periphery to the centre during the late colonial era. However, those profits merely whetted those Creoles' appetites for greater free trade than the Bourbons were willing to grant. More generally, Creoles reacted angrily against the crown's preference for peninsulars in administrative positions and its declining support of the caste system and the Creoles' privileged status within it. After hundreds of years of proven service to Spain, the American-born elites felt that the Bourbons were now treating them like a recently conquered nation.

In cities throughout the region, Creole frustrations increasingly found expression in ideas derived from the Enlightenment. Imperial prohibitions proved unable to stop the flow of potentially subversive English, French, and North American works into the colonies of Latin America. Creole participants in conspiracies against Portugal and Spain at the end of the 18th and the beginning of the 19th century showed familiarity with such European Enlightenment thinkers as Thomas Hobbes, John Locke, Montesquieu, and Jean-Jacques Rousseau. The Enlightenment clearly informed the aims of dissident Creoles and inspired some of the later, great leaders of the independence movements across Latin America.

**31**

Still, these ideas were not, strictly speaking, causes of independence. Creoles selectively adapted rather than simply embraced the thought that had informed revolutions in North America and France. Leaders in Latin America tended to shy away from the more socially radical European doctrines. Moreover, the influence of those ideologies was sharply restricted; with few exceptions only small circles of educated, urban elites had access to Enlightenment thought. At most, foreign ideas helped foster a more questioning attitude toward traditional institutions and authority.

# NAPOLEON'S INVASION OF SPAIN

European diplomatic and military events provided the final catalyst that turned Creole discontent into full-fledged movements for Latin American independence. When the Spanish crown entered into an alliance with France in 1795, it set off a series of developments that opened up economic and political distance between the Iberian countries and their American colonies. By siding with France, Spain pitted itself against England, the dominant sea power of the period, which used its naval forces to reduce and eventually cut communications between Spain and the Americas. Unable to preserve any sort of monopoly on trade, the Spanish crown was forced to loosen the restrictions on its colonies' commerce. Spanish Americans now found themselves able to trade legally with other colonies, as well as with any neutral countries such as the United States. Spain's wartime liberalization of colonial trade sharpened Creoles' desires for greater economic self-determination.

Occurrences in Europe in the early 19th century created a deep political divide between Spain and its

FRANCISCO DE GOYA'S PAINTING THE THIRD OF MAY 1808 DEPICTS THE SPANISH RESISTANCE TO NAPOLEON'S INVASION.

American colonies. In 1807 the Spanish king, Charles IV, granted passage through Spanish territory to Napoleon's forces on their way to invade Portugal. The immediate effect of that concession was to send the Portuguese ruler, Prince Regent John, fleeing in British ships to Brazil. Arriving in Rio de Janeiro with some 15,000 officials, nobles, and other members of his court, John transformed the Brazilian colony into the administrative centre of his empire. When Napoleon turned on his Spanish allies in 1808, events took a disastrous turn for Spain and its dominion in the Americas. Shortly after Charles had abdicated in favour of his son Ferdinand, Napoleon had them both imprisoned. With these figures of legitimate authority in his power, the French ruler tried to shatter Spanish independence. In the process he set off a political crisis that swept across both Spain and its possessions.

The Spanish political tradition centred on the figure of the monarch, yet, with Charles and Ferdinand removed from the scene, the hub of all political authority was missing. Napoleon placed his own brother Joseph Bonaparte on the throne, but the Bonaparte government faced opposition from patriotic juntas in Spain in the name of the exiled Ferdinand VII and aided by the British. In most of Spanish America there was general sympathy with the regency, but both claims were rejected, mainly on the ground that an interregnum existed and thus, under ancient principles of Spanish law, the king's dominions in America had the right to govern themselves pending the restoration of a lawful king.

# CARETAKER GOVERNMENTS

In 1810 a Cortes (Parliament) emerged in Cádiz to represent both Spain and Spanish America. Two years later it produced a new, liberal constitution that proclaimed Spain's American possessions to be full members of the kingdom and not mere colonies. Yet the Creoles who participated in the new Cortes were denied equal representation. Moreover, the Cortes would not concede permanent free trade to the Americans and obstinately refused to grant any degree of meaningful autonomy to the overseas dominions. Having had a taste of freedom during their political and economic isolation from the mother country, Spanish Americans did not easily consent to a reduction of their power and autonomy.

# JUNTAS

A junta (Spanish: "meeting") is a committee or administrative council, particularly one that rules a country after a coup d'état and before a legal government has been established. The word was widely used in the 16th century to refer to numerous government consultative committees. The Spanish resistance to Napoleon's invasion (1808) was organized by the *juntas provinciales*; the national committee was the *junta suprema central*. Around the same time, many of Spain's Latin American colonies formed juntas that claimed loyalty to Ferdinand VII, Spain's exiled ruler. However, in practice these juntas represented the establishment of autonomous governments. In subsequent civil wars or revolutionary disturbances in Spain, Greece, or Latin America, similar bodies, elected or self-appointed, have usually been called juntas.

Two other European developments further dashed the hopes of Creoles, pushing them more decisively toward independence. The year 1814 saw the restoration of Ferdinand to the throne and with it the energetic attempt to reestablish Spanish imperial power in the Americas. Rejecting compromise and reform, Ferdinand resorted to military force to bring wayward Spanish-American regions back into the empire as colonies. The effort only served to harden the position of Creole rebels. In 1820 troops waiting in Cádiz to be sent as part of the crown's military campaigns revolted, forcing Ferdinand to agree to a series of liberal measures. That concession divided and weakened loyalist opposition to independence in the Americas. Many supporters of the crown now had doubts about the monarchy for which they were fighting.

Creoles and peninsulars began to jockey for power across Spanish America. During 1808–10 juntas emerged to rule in the name of Ferdinand VII. In Mexico City and Montevideo caretaker governments were the work of loyal peninsular Spaniards eager to head off Creole threats. In Santiago, Caracas, Bogotá, and other cities, by contrast, it was Creoles who controlled the provisional juntas. Not all of these governments lasted very long; loyalist troops quickly put down Creole-dominated juntas in La Paz and Quito. By 1810, however, the trend was clear. Without denouncing Ferdinand, Creoles throughout most of the region were moving toward the establishment of their own autonomous governments. Transforming these early initiatives into a break with Spanish control required tremendous sacrifice. Over the next decade and a half, Spanish Americans had to defend with arms their movement toward independence.

The movements that liberated Spanish South America arose from opposite ends of the continent. From the north came the movement led most famously by Simón Bolívar, a dynamic figure known as the Liberator. From the south proceeded another powerful force, this one directed by the more circumspect José de San Martín. After difficult conquests of their home regions, the two movements spread the cause of independence through other territories, finally meeting on the central Pacific coast. From there, troops under northern generals finally stamped out the last vestiges of loyalist resistance in Peru and Bolivia by 1826.

# CHAPTER 3

# THE SOUTHERN
# MOVEMENT IN
# SOUTH AMERICA

The struggles that produced independence in the south began even before Napoleon's invasion of Portugal and Spain. In 1806 a British expeditionary force captured Buenos Aires. When the Spanish colonial officials proved ineffective against the invasion, a volunteer militia of Creoles and peninsulars organized resistance and pushed the British out in two battles known as the Reconquista and the Defensa.

The *cabildo*, or municipal council, was the only organ that had given the colonists experience in self-government. Though its powers were very limited, this ancient Spanish institution had existed in all the colonies since the 16th century. In emergencies it was converted into an "open" *cabildo*, a kind of town meeting, which included prominent members of the community. On May 25, 1810 (now celebrated in Argentina as Venticinco de Mayo, the day of the revolution), such an open

*THIS PAINTING BY JUAN MANUEL BLANES SHOWS THE CABILDO IN ARGENTINA ON MAY 22, 1810, THREE DAYS BEFORE IT ESTABLISHED ITS OWN GOVERNMENT AND ESSENTIALLY DECLARED INDEPENDENCE FROM SPAIN.*

*cabildo* in Buenos Aires established an autonomous government to administer the Viceroyalty of the Río de la Plata in the name of Ferdinand VII, pending his restoration. Although shielding itself with a pretense of loyalty to Ferdinand, the junta produced by that session marked the end of Spanish rule in Buenos Aires and its hinterland. After its revolution of May 1810, the region was the only one to resist reconquest by loyalist troops throughout the period of the independence wars.

# TROUBLE IN AND AROUND BUENOS AIRES

Independence in the former Viceroyalty of the Río de la Plata, however, encountered grave difficulties in the years after 1810. Central authority proved unstable in the capital city of Buenos Aires. An early radical liberal government dominated by Mariano Moreno gave way to a series of triumvirates and supreme directors. More troubling still were the bitter rivalries emerging between Buenos Aires and other provinces. From the start Buenos Aires' intention of bringing all the former viceregal territories under its control set off waves of discord in the outlying provinces. At stake was not only political autonomy per se but also economic interest; the Creole merchants of Buenos Aires, who initially sought the liberalization of colonial restraints on commerce in the region, subsequently tried to maintain their economic dominance over the interior. A constituent assembly meeting in 1813 adopted a flag, anthem, and other symbols of national identity, but the apparent unity disintegrated soon afterward. This was evident in the assembly that finally proclaimed independence on July 9, 1816 (Nueve de Julio) under the name of the United Provinces of the Río de la Plata; that body received no delegates from several provinces, even though it was held outside Buenos Aires, in the interior city of Tucumán (in full, San Miguel de Tucumán).

Distinct interests and long-standing resentment of the viceregal capital led different regions in the south to pursue separate destinies. Across the Río de la Plata from Buenos Aires, Montevideo and its surroundings became the separate Estado Oriental ("Eastern State," later Uruguay). Caught between the loyalism of Spanish officers and the imperialist intentions of Buenos Aires and Portuguese Brazil, the regional leader José Gervasio Artigas formed an army of thousands of gauchos. By 1815 Artigas and this force dominated Uruguay and had allied with other provinces to oppose Buenos Aires.

Buenos Aires achieved similarly mixed results in other neighbouring regions, losing control of many while spreading independence from Spain. Paraguay resisted Buenos Aires' military and set out on a path of relative isolation from the outside world. Other expeditions took the cause to Upper Peru, the region that would become Bolivia. After initial victories there, the forces from Buenos Aires retreated, leaving the battle in the hands of local Creole, mestizo, and Indian guerrillas. By the time Bolívar's armies finally completed the liberation of Upper Peru (then renamed in the Liberator's honour), the region had long since separated itself from Buenos Aires.

## *LA PATRIA VIEJA* IN CHILE

In Chile the initial move toward independence was made on Sept. 18, 1810, when a *cabildo abierto* (open town meeting) in Santiago, attended by representatives of privileged groups whose vaguely defined objectives included a change in administration, accepted the resignation of the President-Governor and in his place elected a junta composed of local leaders.

From 1810 to 1813 the course of the patriots was relatively peaceful because they were able to maintain themselves without formal ties to the Viceroyalty of Lima. Trade restrictions were relaxed; steps were taken toward the eventual abolition of slavery; a newspaper was established to publicize the beliefs of the patriots; and education was promoted, including the founding of the National Institute. However, the embers of civil strife were also fanned. The Creoles were divided over how far the colony should go toward self-government. José Miguel Carrera and his brothers, whose desire for complete independence was equaled if not surpassed by their personal ambition, inflamed the issues. Meanwhile, Spain had taken steps to reassert its control over the colony. At the Battle of Rancagua, on Oct. 1 and 2, 1814, it reestablished its military supremacy and ended what has been called *la patria vieja* ("the old fatherland").

Following the defeat at Rancagua, patriot leaders, among them the Carrera brothers and Bernardo O'Higgins, future director-dictator of Chile, migrated to Argentina. There O'Higgins won the support of José de San Martín, who, with the support of the revolutionary government in Buenos Aires, was raising an army to free the southern portion of the continent by first liberating Chile and then attacking Peru from the sea. The Carreras continued their spirited agitation for independence in Buenos Aires and the United States.

## CAMPAIGN ACROSS THE ANDES

José de San Martín, who became one of the most important revolutionary leaders in South America, distinguished himself as a trainer and leader of soldiers in the service of the Buenos Aires government. After winning a skirmish against loyalist forces at San Lorenzo, on the right bank of the Paraná River (Feb. 3, 1813), he was sent to Tucumán to reinforce, and ultimately replace, General Manuel Belgrano, who was being hard pressed by forces of the viceroy of Peru. San Martín recognized that the Río de la Plata provinces would never be secure so long as the royalists held Lima, but he perceived the military impossibility of reaching the centre of viceregal power by way of the conventional overland route through Upper Peru (modern Bolivia). He therefore quietly prepared the masterstroke that was his supreme contribution to the liberation of southern South America. First, he disciplined and trained the army around Tucumán so that, with the assistance of gaucho *guerrilleros*, they would be capable of a holding operation. Then, on the pretense of ill health, he got himself appointed governor intendant of the province of Cuyo, the capital of which was Mendoza, the key to the routes across the Andes. There, he set about creating an army that would link up overland with the soldiers of the patriotic government in Chile and then proceed by sea to attack Peru.

# JOSÉ DE SAN MARTÍN'S EARLY LIFE

José de San Martín was an Argentine soldier, statesman, and national hero who helped lead the revolutions against Spanish rule in Argentina (1812), Chile (1818), and Peru (1821).

San Martín's father, Juan de San Martín, a professional soldier, was administrator of Yapeyú, formerly a Jesuit mission station in Guaraní Indian territory, on the northern frontier of Argentina. His mother, Gregoria Matorras, was also Spanish. The family returned to Spain when José was six. From 1785 to 1789 he was educated at the Seminary of Nobles in Madrid, leaving there to begin his military career as a cadet in the Murcia infantry regiment. For the next 20 years he was a loyal officer of the Spanish monarch, fighting against

(*continued on page 45*)

Nada profirió mas que la Libertad de su Patria.

THE INSCRIPTION ON THE BOTTOM LEFT CORNER OF THIS PORTRAIT OF JOSÉ DE SAN MARTÍN READS "HE WOULD PREFER NOTHING MORE THAN THE FREEDOM OF HIS COUNTRY" IN SPANISH.

# JOSÉ DE SAN MARTÍN'S EARLY LIFE
(CONTINUED)

the Moors in Oran (1791); against the British (1798), who held him captive for more than a year; and against the Portuguese in the War of the Oranges (1801). He was made captain in 1804.

The turning point in San Martín's career came in 1808, following Napoleon's occupation of Spain and the subsequent patriotic uprising against the French there. For two years he served the Sevilla (Seville) junta that was conducting the war on behalf of the imprisoned Spanish king Ferdinand VII. He was promoted to the rank of lieutenant colonel for his conduct in the Battle of Bailén (1808) and was elevated to command of the Sagunto Dragoons after the Battle of Albuera (1811). Instead of taking up his new post, he sought permission to go to Lima, the capital of the viceroyalty of Peru, but traveled by way of London to Buenos Aires, which had become the principal centre of resistance in South America to the Sevilla junta and its successor, the Cádiz-based Council of Regency. There, in the year 1812, San Martín was given the task of organizing a corps of grenadiers against the Spanish royalists centred in Peru who threatened the revolutionary government in Argentina.

One possible explanation for this startling change of allegiance on the part of a soldier who had sworn fealty to Spain is that it was prompted by British sympathizers with the independence movement in Spanish America and that San Martín was recruited through the agency of James Duff, 4th Earl of Fife, who had fought in Spain (and who caused San Martín to be made a freeman of Banff, Scotland). In later years, San Martín averred that he had sacrificed his career in Spain because he had responded to the call of his native land, and this is the view taken by Argentinian historians. Undoubtedly, peninsular Spanish prejudice against anyone born in the Indies must have rankled throughout his career in Spain and caused him to identify himself with the Creole revolutionaries.

To his disappointment, when the first stage of this plan was nearing completion, loyalist forces recaptured Chile (although the Chilean liberator, Bernardo O'Higgins, was able to escape to Mendoza). This made it necessary for San Martín to fight his way westward across the formidable barrier of the Andes. This was accomplished between Jan. 18 and Feb. 8, 1817, partly by a double bluff, which caused the Spanish commander to divide his forces in order to guard all possible routes, and more especially by careful generalship that ensured the maximum concentration of force at the enemy's weakest point, backed by adequate supplies. San Martín's skill in leading his men through the defiles, chasms, and passes—often 10,000 to 12,000 feet (3,000 to 4,000 meters) above sea level—of the Andean cordillera has caused him to be ranked with Hannibal and Napoleon. On February 12 he surprised and defeated the royalists at Casas de Chacabuco and took Santiago, where he refused the offer of the governorship of Chile in favour of O'Higgins (who became supreme director) because he did not wish to be diverted from his main objective, the capture of Lima. Nevertheless, it took him more than a year to clear the country of royalist troops. He finally routed the principal remaining armies, some 5,000, on April 5, 1818, at the Battle of Maipú. Chile's independence was officially declared on the first anniversary of Chacabuco, Feb. 12, 1818.

The next stage of San Martín's plan involved the creation of the Chilean navy and the accumulation of troop ships. This was accomplished, despite a shortage of funds, by August 1820, when the rather shoddy fleet, consisting mainly of armed merchant ships, under the command of Thomas Cochrane (later 10th Earl of Dundonald), left Valparaíso for the Peruvian coast. Cochrane, whom San Martín found a cantankerous colleague, had failed the year before to take the chief port, Callao, which was well-defended. The port was therefore blockaded, and the troops were landed to the south near Pisco; from this point they could threaten Lima from the landward side. True to his cautious nature, San Martín resisted the temptation to assault the capital, which was defended by a superior force, and waited for almost a year, until the royalists, despairing of assistance from Ferdinand VII (who had since been restored to the Spanish throne), withdrew to the mountains. San Martín and his army then entered Lima, the independence of Peru was proclaimed on July 28, 1821, and the victorious revolutionary commander was made protector.

## THE GUAYAQUIL CONFERENCE

San Martín's position was nevertheless insecure. He had broken with his supporters in Buenos Aires when, against their wishes, he insisted on pressing on to Lima; he was unsure of the backing of some of his officers, many of whom suspected him of dictatorial or monarchical ambitions; and he lacked the forces to subdue the royalist remnants in the interior. Having benefited from colonial monopolies and fearful of the kind of social violence that the late 18th-century revolt had threatened, many Peruvian Creoles were not anxious to break with Spain. Moreover, Simón Bolívar, who had liberated the northern provinces of South America, had annexed Guayaquil, a port and province that San Martín had hoped would opt for incorporation in Peru. He therefore decided to confront Bolívar.

The two victorious generals met on July 26, 1822, in Guayaquil, where Bolívar had already taken control. Details

*The historic meeting between Bolívar and San Martín is remembered in this statue of the two men in Guayaquil.*

of their discussions are not known, but presumably they covered completion of the military struggle in Peru as well as the subsequent organization of liberated Hispanic America. San Martín must have understood that Bolívar alone combined the military, political, and psychological assets needed to gain final victory over the powerful Spanish army in the highlands. Given the situation in Lima, where he faced mounting opposition, San Martín's presence there could only hinder the performance of that task. There, seriously ill, faced by recriminations and overt disaffection, he resigned his protectorship on September 20. In a message to the Peruvian Congress he left a farsighted warning: "The presence of a successful soldier (no matter how disinterested) is dangerous to the States that have just been constituted."

San Martín's contribution to the cause of independence was his military skill. The boldness of his plan to attack the viceroyalty of Lima by crossing the Andes to Chile and going on by sea, as well as the patience and determination with which he executed it, was undoubtedly the decisive factor in the defeat of Spanish power in southern South America. Whether at Guayaquil he consciously made a great renunciation of personal ambition so that Bolívar, and with him the cause of independence, might triumph, or whether he went into voluntary exile because Bolívar made it clear that he was not prepared to help Peru so long as San Martín remained in control, remains an unresolved historical problem. The rest of his life was spent in exile with his daughter, in Brussels, Paris, and Boulogne-sur-Mer, wisely avoiding any further involvement in the anarchic situations that marred the early history of the newly independent nations. He died in Boulogne-sur-Mer in 1850.

# INDEPENDENCE IN THE SOUTH

As the independence movements grew, the Buenos Aires government tried to maintain the integrity of the old Viceroyalty of the Río de la Plata, but the outlying portions, never effectively controlled, soon were lost: Paraguay in 1814, Bolivia in 1825, and Uruguay in 1828.

## PARAGUAY

As the power of Buenos Aires grew, the leaders of Paraguay began to resent the decline in their province's significance, and, although they had early challenged Spanish authority, they refused to accept the declaration of Argentine independence in 1810 as applying to Paraguay. Nor could an Argentine army under General Manuel Belgrano enforce Paraguayan acceptance, as Paraguayan militia repulsed Belgrano's forces in 1811. Later, however, when the Spanish governor sought assistance from the Portuguese in defending the colony from further attacks from Buenos Aires, he underestimated the nationalistic spirit of the Paraguayans. Under the leadership of the militia captains Pedro Juan Cabellero and Fulgencio Yegros, they promptly deposed the governor and declared their independence on May 14, 1811.

A governing junta was soon established, led by militia captain Fulgencio Yegros but in reality dominated by a civilian lawyer, José Gaspar Rodríguez de Francia. Francia proposed the idea of a confederation of equals to Buenos Aires. The city was hoping for eventual domination but settled for a vague military alliance, which was signed in October 1811. This constituted de facto recognition of Paraguayan independence, and, when Buenos Aires attempted to use the alliance to acquire Paraguayan troops for its own interprovincial quarrels, the accord became void. Buenos Aires's response was to blockade Paraguay. In the face of regional fragmentation, Buenos Aires sent Nicolás de Herrera to Asunción to frighten, bluff, or bribe Paraguay into a union of unequals. Francia responded by convening a congress, which on Oct. 12, 1813, formally declared Paraguay an independent republic and rejected further treaties with Buenos Aires.

## BOLIVIA

In 1809 Chuquisaca and La Paz became two of the earliest cities to rebel against the colonial government appointed by the new Napoleonic ruler of Spain. Many historians have considered this action to be the beginning of the wars of independence in Latin America. Although viceregal authorities in Lima quickly put down the rebellions, similar uprisings were successful in the viceregal capital of Buenos Aires. From that city several revolutionary armies were dispatched without success to liberate Upper Peru; however, the guerrilla units formed in the rugged countryside of Upper Peru kept the revolutionary movements alive for some 16 years.

In 1825 an army under the leadership of Marshal Antonio José de Sucre liberated Upper Peru with the aid of defecting royalists, who were mostly Creole elites. The defectors convinced Bolívar and Sucre to allow autonomy for Upper Peru rather than union with either Peru or Argentina, and on Aug. 6, 1825, an Upper Peruvian congress declared the country independent. Few of the guerrilla commanders, representing a more humble constituency, were able to become part of the Creole elite–led government.

## URUGUAY

Montevideo, with its Spanish military and naval contingents, was a royalist stronghold when a movement for independence broke out in Buenos Aires in 1810. In the interior of the Banda Oriental, the fight against Spain was led from 1811 by José Gervasio Artigas, commander of the Blandengues, a mounted corps that the Spaniards had originally created to police the region. Artigas's small army, which soon included a battalion of freed African slaves, was supported by rural inhabitants, antiroyalist Montevideo leaders, and an army from Buenos Aires. Following victories in the interior and in Montevideo, Artigas promoted a loose confederation of provinces of la Plata, but he also considered forming a rival confederation centring on Montevideo. These plans, coupled with Artigas's growing power and egalitarian policies (including redistributing *estanciero* land to freed slaves and other poor Uruguayans), made him a threat to elites in Uruguay and centralists in Buenos Aires, who acquiesced when Portuguese Brazilian forces took over the Banda Oriental in 1820, and Artigas was driven into exile.

"Brazilianization" was resisted within the Banda Oriental and by Uruguayan exiles as well. Argentines felt increasingly threatened by the Brazilian presence, and their government was compelled to support Juan Antonio Lavalleja, one of Artigas's exiled officers, and his "33 *orientales*" when

*THIS EQUESTRIAN STATUE OF JOSÉ GERVASIO ARTIGAS STANDS IN PLAZA INDEPENDENCIA IN MONTEVIDEO, NOW THE CAPITAL OF URUGUAY.*

they crossed the river to free their homeland in 1825. The ensuing war was a stalemate, but British diplomats mediated a settlement in 1827, and in 1828 a treaty was ratified creating Uruguay as a separate state and a buffer between Brazil and Argentina; the nation's strategic location also served British interests by guaranteeing that the Río de la Plata would remain an international waterway. On July 18, 1830, when the constitution for the Oriental State of Uruguay was approved, the country had scarcely 74,000 inhabitants.

# THE NORTH AND THE CULMINATION OF INDEPENDENCE

I ndependence movements in the northern regions of Spanish South America had a few false starts. A group of Venezuelan Creoles boldly proclaimed their country an independent republic in 1797. Although their effort failed, it forewarned of the revolutionary movements that were soon to inflame Latin America. The small group of foreign volunteers from New York City that the Venezuelan revolutionary Francisco de Miranda brought to his homeland failed to incite the populace to rise against Spanish rule. Creoles in the region wanted an expansion of the free trade that was benefiting their plantation economy. At the same time, however, they feared that the removal of Spanish control might bring about a revolution that would destroy their own power.

Creole elites had good reason to fear such a possibility, for a massive slave revolution had recently exploded in the French Caribbean colony of Saint-Domingue, which became

**55**

the independent nation of Haiti. Partly inspired by those Caribbean events, slaves in Venezuela carried out their own uprisings in the 1790s. Just as it served as a beacon of hope for the enslaved, Haiti was a warning of everything that might go wrong for elites in the cacao-growing areas of Venezuela and throughout slave societies in the Americas.

# INDEPENDENCE DECLARED IN COLOMBIA AND VENEZUELA

Creole anxieties contributed to the persistence of strong loyalist factions in the Viceroyalty of New Granada, but they did not prevent the rise of an independence struggle there. Creoles organized revolutionary governments that proclaimed some social and economic reforms in 1810. The uprising in Bogotá on July 20, 1810, is commemorated as Independence Day in Colombia, although these new governments swore allegiance to Ferdinand VII and did not begin to declare independence until 1811.

In Venezuela, forces loyal to Spain fought the patriots from the start, leading to a pattern in which patriot rebels held the capital city and its surroundings but could not dominate large areas of the countryside. On April 19, 1810, the Spanish governor was officially deprived of his powers and expelled from Venezuela. A junta took over. To obtain help, Simón Bolívar was sent on a mission to London, where he arrived in July. His assignment was to explain to England the plight of the revolutionary colony, to gain recognition for it, and to obtain arms and support. Although he failed in his official negotiations, he did foster the cause of the revolution by persuading the exiled Francisco de Miranda to return to Caracas and to assume command of the independence movement.

In March 1811 a national congress met in Caracas to draft a constitution. After long deliberation it declared Venezuela's independence on July 5, 1811. Bolívar now entered the army of the young republic and was placed in charge of Puerto Cabello, a port vital to Venezuela. Treasonable action by one of Bolívar's officers opened the fortress to the Spanish forces, and Miranda, the commander in chief, entered into negotiations with the Spanish commander in chief. An armistice was signed (July 1812) that left the entire country at the mercy of Spain. Miranda was turned over to the Spaniards—after Bolívar and others prevented his escape from Venezuela—and spent the rest of his life in Spanish dungeons. Some saw the earthquake that wreaked particular destruction in patriot-held areas in 1812 as a sign of divine displeasure with the revolution.

Determined to continue the struggle, Bolívar obtained a passport to leave the country and went to Cartagena in New Granada (the heart of the viceroyalty). There he published the first of his great political statements, "El Manifiesto de Cartagena," in which he attributed the fall of the First Republic to the lack of strong government and called for a united revolutionary effort to destroy the power of Spain in America.

Bolívar soon returned to Venezuela with a new army in 1813 and waged a campaign with a ferocity that is captured perfectly by the army's motto, "Guerra a muerte" ("War to the death"). In a sweeping, hard-fought campaign, he vanquished the royalists in six pitched battles and on Aug. 6, 1813, entered Caracas. He was given the title of Liberator and assumed political dictatorship. But the war of independence was just beginning. With loyalists displaying the same passion and violence, as well as obtaining significant support from the common people of mixed ethnicity, the revolutionists achieved only short-lived victories. The army led by loyalist José Tomás Boves demonstrated the key military role that the *llaneros* (cowboys) came to play in the region's struggle. Turning the tide against independence, these highly mobile, ferocious fighters made up a formidable military force. Boves subjected Creole patriots to terrible atrocities, and his capture of Caracas and other principal cities ended the second Venezuelan republic. Narrowly escaping Miranda's fate, Bolívar fled to New Granada and eventually Jamaica.

# SIMÓN BOLÍVAR'S EARLY LIFE

Simón Bolívar, known as The Liberator, was a South American soldier and statesman who led the revolutions against Spanish rule in the Viceroyalty of New Granada. He was president of Gran Colombia (1819-30) and dictator of Peru (1823-26). Hero and symbol of South American independence, Bolívar did not produce victory by himself, of course; still, he was of fundamental importance to the movement as an ideologue, military leader, and political catalyst.

The son of a Venezuelan aristocrat of Spanish descent, Bolívar was born to wealth and position on July 24, 1783, in Caracas, New Granada (now Venezuela). After his father died when the boy was three years old and his mother died six years later, his uncle administered his inheritance and provided him with tutors. At the age of 16, Bolívar was sent to Europe to complete his education. For three years he lived in Spain and in 1801 married the daughter of a Spanish nobleman, with whom he returned to Caracas. The young bride died of yellow fever less than a year after her marriage. In 1804,

(*continued on page 60*)

*Simón Bolívar is shown in a detail of an engraving by C.G. Childs.*

# SIMÓN BOLÍVAR'S EARLY LIFE
(CONTINUED)

when Napoleon was approaching the pinnacle of his career, Bolívar returned to Europe. In Paris he encountered a former childhood tutor, Simón Rodríguez, who guided him to the writings of European rationalist thinkers such as Locke, Hobbes, Buffon, d'Alembert, and Helvetius as well as Voltaire, Montesquieu, and Rousseau. The idea of independence for Hispanic America took root in Bolívar's imagination, and, on a trip to Rome, standing on the heights of the Monte Sacro, he made a vow to liberate his country.

In 1807 he returned to Venezuela by way of the United States, visiting the eastern cities. The Latin American independence movement was launched a year after Bolívar's return, as Napoleon's invasion of Spain unsettled Spanish authority. Bolívar participated in various conspiratorial meetings from the beginning, immediately establishing himself as a crucial figure in the fight for independence.

## THE JAMAICA LETTER

In exile, Bolívar wrote the greatest document of his career: "La Carta de Jamaica" ("The Letter from Jamaica"), in which he outlined a grandiose panorama from Chile and Argentina to Mexico. "The bonds," wrote Bolívar, "that united us to Spain have been severed." Bolívar affirmed his undying faith in the cause of independence, even in the face of the patriots' repeated defeats. While laying out sharp criticisms of Spanish colonialism, the document also looked toward the future. For Bolívar, the only path for the former colonies was the establishment of autonomous, centralized republican government. He proposed constitutional republics throughout Hispanic America, and for the former Viceroyalty of New Granada he envisioned a government modeled on that of Great Britain, with a hereditary upper house, an elected lower house, and a president chosen for life. The last provision, to which Bolívar clung throughout his career, constituted the most dubious feature of his political thinking.

Although liberal in some respects, in the Jamaica Letter and elsewhere, he expressed strong doubts about the capacity of his fellow Latin Americans for self-government, revealing his socially conservative and politically authoritarian side. "Do not adopt the best system of government," he wrote, "but the one most likely to succeed." Thus, the type of republic that he eventually espoused was very much an oligarchic one, with socioeconomic and literacy qualifications for suffrage and with power centred in the hands of a strong executive. And though he favoured the granting of civil liberties to all male citizens and the abolition of slavery, Bolívar also worried that the death of so many peninsular soldiers during the wars would condemn Latin America to a system of "pardocracy," or rule by *pardos* (people of mixed ethnicity), an outcome he deemed threatening. He believed that a virtuous governing system would not be possible if the nation was divided by ethnicity.

# LIBERATION OF NEW GRANADA

By 1815 the independence movements in Venezuela and almost all across Spanish South America seemed to be declining. Spain had sent to its rebellious colonies the strongest expeditionary force that had ever crossed the Atlantic. Its commander was Pablo Morillo, who administered the region in a heavy-handed fashion, however, and many of the Creole elites who had initially supported him soon conspired for his defeat. *Llaneros* and blacks also deserted the royalist cause and joined Bolívar, whose army was further augmented by a legion of British and Irish mercenaries; Haiti also sent money and weapons after Bolívar visited the republic.

The Liberator emerged as a strong military and political force in the struggles that began in 1817. At this point he expanded the focus of the movement, shifting his attention to New Granada and courting supporters among the *casta* majority. He decided to set up headquarters in the Orinoco region, which had not been devastated by war and from which the Spaniards could not easily oust him. He engaged the services of several thousand foreign soldiers and officers, mostly British and Irish, established his capital at Angostura (now Ciudad Bolívar), and began to publish a newspaper. He also established liaison with the revolutionary forces of the plains, including one group led by José Antonio Páez and another group led by Francisco de Paula Santander. Páez's *llaneros* of mixed ethnicity proved crucial to the patriots' military victories in 1818–19.

In spring 1819 Bolívar conceived his master plan of attacking the Viceroyalty of New Granada. Bolívar's attack on New Granada will always be considered one of the most daring in military history. The route of the small army (about 2,500 men, including the British legion) led through flood-swept plains and icy mountains, over routes that the Spanish considered nearly impassable. The Spaniards were taken by surprise, and in the crucial Battle of Boyacá on Aug. 7, 1819, the bulk of the royalist army surrendered to Bolívar. Three days later he entered Bogotá. This was the turning point in the history of northern South America.

# CREATION OF GRAN COLOMBIA

Consolidating victory in the north proved difficult. A congress that Bolívar had convened in Angostura in 1819 named the Liberator president and military dictator of Gran Colombia, a union of what are today Venezuela, Colombia, Panama, and Ecuador. In reality, sharp divisions permeated the region even before Angostura; these ultimately dashed Bolívar's hopes of uniting the former Spanish colonies into a single new nation. The Bogotá area, for example, had previously refused to join in a confederation with the rest of revolutionary New Granada. Furthermore, loyalist supporters still held much of Venezuela, parts of the Colombian Andes, and all of Ecuador. Still, the tide had turned in favour of independence.

Early in 1820 a revolution in Spain forced the Spanish king to recognize the ideals of liberalism on the home front, an action that discouraged the Spanish forces in South America. Bolívar persuaded Morillo to open armistice negotiations, and the two warriors met in a memorable encounter at Santa Ana, signing in November 1820 a treaty that ended hostilities for a six-month period. When fighting was resumed, Bolívar found it easy, with his superior manpower, to defeat the Spanish forces in Venezuela. The Battle of Carabobo (June 1821) opened the gates of Caracas, and Bolívar's Venezuelan homeland was at last free.

In the autumn of the same year a congress convened in Cúcuta to draft a constitution for Gran Colombia as a centralized representative government. Prior to that time the government was highly military and hierarchically organized, with regional vice presidents exercising direct power while its president, Bolívar, was campaigning. Bolívar remained president, but the new constitution disappointed him. He thought the constitution too liberal in character to guarantee the survival of his creation. As long as more urgent assignments claimed his attention, however, he was willing to put up with its weak structure.

Leaving his trusted right-hand man, Santander, in Bogotá to rule the new government, Bolívar then pushed on into Ecuador and the central Andes. In this campaign Bolívar was assisted by the most brilliant of his officers, Antonio José de Sucre. While Bolívar engaged the Spaniards in the mountains that defended the northern access to Quito, capital of Ecuador, Sucre marched from the Pacific coast to the interior. At Pichincha, on May 24, 1822, he won a victory that freed Ecuador from the Spanish yoke. On the following day the capital fell, and Bolívar joined forces with Sucre on June 16.

# LIBERATION OF PERU

The territory of Gran Colombia—comprising present-day Colombia, Venezuela, Ecuador, and Panama—had now been completely recovered from Spain, and its new government was recognized by the United States. Only Peru and Upper Peru remained in the hands of the Spaniards. These areas had remained loyal because of the conservative attitude of the Peruvian aristocracy, the presence of many Spaniards in Peru, the concentration of Spanish military power in Lima, and the effective suppression of Indian uprisings. Peru's independence was, consequently, achieved primarily by outsiders: Bolívar and the Argentine revolutionary José de San Martín.

San Martín had done for the southern part of the continent what Bolívar had accomplished for the north. In addition, he had already entered Lima and proclaimed Peru's independence.

*IN THIS PAINTING, BOLÍVAR LEADS HIS TROOPS INTO THE BATTLE OF JUNÍN ON AUGUST 5, 1824, AS PART OF THE LIBERATION OF PERU.*

But the Spanish forces had retreated into the highlands, and San Martín, unable to follow them, decided to consult with Bolívar. On July 26, 1822, the two men met in the port city of Guayaquil, Ecuador. Accounts of their meeting vary widely, but apparently San Martín made the realistic evaluation that only Bolívar and his supporters could complete the liberation of the Andes. On his return from Guayaquil, San Martín resigned his office in Lima and went into exile, allowing Bolívar to assume sole direction of the war.

From that point on, the northerners took charge of the struggle in Peru and Bolivia. After standing by while Spanish forces threatened to recapture the lands that San Martín's armies had emancipated, Bolívar responded to the calls of Peruvian

Creoles and guided his soldiers to victory in Lima. While he organized the government there, his lieutenants set out to win the highlands of Peru and Upper Peru. Sucre directed the patriots' triumph at Ayacucho in 1824, which turned out to be the last major battle of the war. Within two years independence fighters mopped up the last of loyalist resistance, and South America was free of Spanish control.

Bolívar was now president of Gran Colombia and dictator of Peru. Only a small section of the continent—Upper Peru—was still defended by royalist forces. The liberation of this region fell to Sucre, and in April 1825 he reported that the task had been accomplished. The new nation chose to be called Bolivia after the name of the Liberator. For this child of his genius, Bolívar drafted a constitution that showed once more his authoritarian inclinations: it created a lifetime president, a legislative body consisting of three chambers, and a highly restricted suffrage. Bolívar was devoted to his own creation, but, as the instrument of social reform that he had envisaged, the constitution was a failure.

## UNIFICATION OR NATION-STATES?

Bolívar had now reached the high point of his career. His power extended from the Caribbean to the Argentine-Bolivian border. He had conquered severe illness, which during his sojourn in Peru had made him practically an invalid for months at a time. Another of his favourite projects, a league of Hispanic American states, came to fruition in 1826. He had long advocated treaties of alliance between the American republics, whose weakness he correctly apprehended. By 1824 such treaties had been signed and ratified by the republics of Colombia, Peru, Mexico, Central America, and the United Provinces of the Río de la Plata. In 1826 a general American congress convened in Panama under Bolívar's auspices. Compared with Bolívar's original proposals, it was a fragmentary affair, with only Colombia, Peru, Central America, and Mexico sending representatives. The four nations that attended signed a treaty of alliance and invited all other American nations to adhere to it. A common army and navy were planned, and a biannual assembly representing the federated states was projected. All controversies among the states were to be solved by arbitration. Only Colombia ratified the treaty, yet the congress in Panama provided an important example for future hemispheric solidarity and understanding in South America.

But Bolívar was aware that his plans for hemispheric organization had met with only limited acceptance. His contemporaries thought in terms of individual nation-states, Bolívar in terms of continents. In the field of domestic policy he continued to be an authoritarian republican. He thought of himself as a rallying point and anticipated civil war as soon as his words should no longer be heeded. Such a prophecy, made in 1824, was fulfilled in 1826.

## CIVIL WAR IN GRAN COLOMBIA

Venezuela and New Granada began to chafe at the bonds of their union in Gran Colombia. The protagonists in each country, Páez in Venezuela and Santander in New Granada, opposed each other, and at last civil war broke out. Bolívar left Lima in haste, and most authorities agree that Peru was glad to see the end of his three-year reign and its liberation from Colombian influence. In Bogotá, Bolívar found Santander upholding the constitution of Cúcuta and urging that Páez be punished as a rebel. But Bolívar was determined to preserve the unity of Gran Colombia and was therefore willing to appease Páez, with whom he became reconciled early in 1827. Páez bowed to the supreme authority of the Liberator, and in turn Bolívar promised a new constitution that would remedy Venezuelan grievances. He declared himself dictator of Gran Colombia and called for a national convention that met in April 1828. Bolívar refused to influence the elections, with the result that the liberals under the leadership of Santander gained the majority.

Bolívar had hoped that the constitution of Cúcuta would be revised and presidential authority strengthened, but the liberals blocked any such attempts. A stalemate developed. Arguing that the old constitution was no longer valid and that no new one had taken its place, Bolívar assumed dictatorial powers in Gran Colombia. A group of liberal conspirators invaded the presidential palace on the night of September 25, and Bolívar was saved from the daggers of the assassins only by the quick-wittedness of his wife, Manuela Sáenz.

But, though this attempt on his life had failed, the storm signals increased. Bolívar's precarious health began to fail. Peru invaded Ecuador with the intention of annexing Guayaquil. Once more Sucre saved Ecuador and defeated the Peruvians at Tarqui (1829). A few months later, one of Bolívar's most-honoured generals, José María Córdoba, staged a revolt. It was crushed, but Bolívar was disheartened by the continued ingratitude of his former adherents. As discontent spread, it became clear that no group loved the republic enough to fight for its existence. In the fall of 1829, Venezuela seceded from

*By 1830, Gran Colombia had broken into three separate states that became Venezuela, Colombia, and Ecuador. Panama seceded from Colombia in 1905.*

Gran Colombia. Venezuelans had suffered greater casualties and endured more privations during the wars than did any other Latin American national group, because of the ferocity of battles on their own soil and the large number of Venezuelan troops who carried the struggle to other regions.

Reluctantly, Bolívar realized that his very existence presented a danger to the internal and external peace of the nations that owed their independence to him, and on May 8, 1830, he left Bogotá, planning to take refuge in Europe. Reaching the Atlantic coast, he learned that Sucre, whom he had trained as his successor, had been assassinated. Bolívar's grief was boundless. The projected trip to Europe was canceled, and, at the invitation of a Spanish admirer, Bolívar journeyed to his estate near Santa Marta. Ironically, his life ended in the house of a Spaniard, where, toward the end of 1830, he died of tuberculosis.

By then Ecuador had also seceded from Gran Colombia. New Granada, a country of 1.5 million inhabitants in 1835 encompassing present-day Colombia and Panama, was left on its own. Thus Gran Colombia essentially passed into history with its principal architect.

# MEXICO AND CENTRAL AMERICA

The independence of Mexico, like that of Peru, the other major central area of Spain's American empire, came late. As was the case in Lima, Mexican cities had a powerful segment of Creoles and peninsular Spaniards whom the old imperial system had served well. Mexican Creoles, like those in Peru, had the spectre of a major social uprising to persuade them to cling to Spain and stability for a while longer. For many of the powerful in Mexican society, a break with Spain promised mainly a loss of traditional status and power and possibly social revolution.

However, some of the same issues that influenced South America also contributed to Mexico's tension with Spain. Fed by currents of rationalism from England and Europe, the

Enlightenment in Spain and Mexico spurred the spread of new scientific knowledge and, especially, its application to mining and agriculture. Mexico was also influenced by political liberalism when the American and French revolutions called into question the divine right of kings and by growing militarism when the British and Russians encroached on New Spain's colonial frontiers. Having strung a series of mission-forts across northern Mexico, authorities in Madrid and Mexico augmented the few regular Spanish troops that could be spared from the peninsula by fostering a local militia with special exemptions (*fueros*) granted to Creole (Mexican-born) officers. Thus, an explosive combination resulted from the almost simultaneous appearances of new ideas, guns, and administrative confusion between the old Habsburg and the new Bourbon bureaucracies.

The turmoil of Napoleonic Europe was the immediate background of the move for Mexican independence. Napoleon I occupied Spain in 1808, imprisoned King Ferdinand VII, and placed his own brother, Joseph Bonaparte, on the Spanish throne. Rebelling, the Spanish resurrected their long-defunct Cortes (representative assembly) to govern in the absence of the legitimate king, and, with representation from the overseas realms, the Cortes in 1812 promulgated a liberal constitution in the king's name. The document provided for a constitutional monarch, popular suffrage, a representative government, and other features taken from the French and U.S. constitutions. But as Spain sent contradictory commands to Mexico, it stimulated rivalries and revolts. The viceregal establishment put down sporadic rebellions by those who professed loyalty to the imprisoned king but who demanded some form of self-government.

# EARLY INDEPENDENCE MOVEMENTS

What was unique to the Mexican case was that the popular rebellion that exploded in 1810 was actually the first major call for independence in the region. Between 1808 and 1810, peninsulars had acted aggressively to preserve Spain's power in the region. Rejecting the notion of a congress that would address the question of governance in the absence of the Spanish king,

*MEXICO CELEBRATES ITS INDEPENDENCE DAY ON SEPTEMBER 16, THE ANNIVERSARY OF MIGUEL HIDALGO'S CALL TO ARMS IN 1810.*

leading peninsulars in Mexico City deposed the viceroy and persecuted Creoles. They then welcomed weaker viceroys whom they knew they could dominate.

Peninsulars' efforts could not, however, prevent the emergence of an independence struggle. In 1810 the Bajío region produced a unique movement led by a radical priest, Miguel Hidalgo y Costilla. When officials discovered the conspiracy that Hidalgo and other Creoles had been planning in Querétaro, the priest appealed directly to the indigenous and mestizo populace. A rich agricultural and mining zone, the Bajío had recently undergone difficult economic times that hit those rural and urban workers particularly hard. Thus many of them responded eagerly to Hidalgo. On Sept. 16, 1810—the date now celebrated as Mexican Independence Day—Hidalgo issued the "Grito de Dolores" ("Cry of Dolores"), calling for the end of rule by Spanish peninsulars, for equality of races, and for redistribution of land. Although framed as an appeal for resistance to the peninsulars, the Grito was in effect a call for independence.

The enthusiasm that Hidalgo stirred among Indians and mestizos shocked and frightened both Creole and peninsular elites. Warning that the Spaniards would deliver Mexico to the "godless" French, Hidalgo exhorted his followers to fight and die for the Mexican Virgin, Our Lady of Guadalupe. When Hidalgo left his tiny village, he marched with his followers into Guanajuato, a major colonial mining centre peopled by Spaniards and Creoles. There the leading citizens barricaded themselves in a public granary. Hidalgo captured the granary on September 28, but he quickly lost control of his rebel army, which massacred most of the Creole elite and pillaged the town. Hidalgo's untrained army grew to have some 80,000

*JOSÉ MARÍA MORELOS Y PAVÓN BROUGHT ORGANIZATION AND REFORM TO THE MEXICAN INDEPENDENCE MOVEMENT IN 1814, BUT THE REVOLUTION STALLED AFTER HE DIED THE NEXT YEAR.*

members as it conquered towns and larger cities and ultimately threatened Mexico City itself. The movement for independence was becoming a race and class war.

Perhaps fearing the atrocities his troops might commit there, Hidalgo prevented the movement from entering Mexico City. Shortly afterward troops of the viceregal government caught up with the rebels. After a dramatic military defeat, Hidalgo was captured in early 1811 and executed on July 31, ending the first of the political civil wars that were to wrack Mexico for three-fourths of a century.

The death of its first leader did not mean the end of Mexico's first independence campaign. Soon another priest, the mestizo José María Morelos y Pavón took over the reins of the movement. With a small but disciplined rebel army he won control of substantial sections of southern Mexico. The constituent congresses, which Morelos called at Chilpancingo in 1813, issued at Apatzingán in 1814 formal declarations of independence and drafted republican constitutions for the areas under his military control. Under Morelos the rebellion gained clearer objectives of independence and social and economic reform as well as greater organization and a wider social base.

At about the same time, Napoleonic troops were withdrawing from Spain, and in 1814 Ferdinand VII returned from involuntary exile. One of his first acts was to nullify Spain's liberal 1812 constitution. Spanish troops, which were no longer needed to fight the French, were ordered to crush the Morelos revolution. Captured and defrocked, Morelos was shot as a heretic and a revolutionary on Dec. 22, 1815. Scattered but dwindling guerrilla bands kept alive the populist, republican, nationalist tradition of Hidalgo and Morelos. With the defeat and death of Morelos in 1815, the potential national scope of the movement came to an effective end. Although smaller forces under leaders like Vicente Guerrero and Guadalupe Victoria (Manuel Félix Fernández) continued to harass the powerful through guerrilla warfare in several regions, the popular movement for independence in Mexico was no longer a grave threat to elite power.

# THE IGUALA PLAN

Final independence, in fact, was not the result of the efforts of Hidalgo, Morelos, or the forces that had made up their independence drive. It came instead almost by accident when constitutionalists in Spain led a rebellion that, in 1820, forced Ferdinand VII to reinstate the liberal constitution of 1812. Conservatives in Mexico, alarmed that anticlerical liberals would threaten their religious, economic, and social privileges, saw independence from Spain as a method of sparing New Spain from such changes.

Two figures from the early rebellion played central roles in liberating Mexico. One, Guerrero, had been an insurgent chief; the other, Agustín de Iturbide, had been an officer in the campaign against the popular independence movement. The two came together behind an agreement known as the Iguala Plan. Centred on provisions of independence, respect for the Roman Catholic Church, and equality between Mexicans and peninsulars, the plan gained the support of many Creoles, Spaniards, and former rebels. It stipulated further that Mexico would become a constitutional monarchy under Ferdinand VII, that he or some Spanish prince would occupy the throne in Mexico City, and that an interim junta would draw up regulations for the election of deputies to a congress that would write a constitution for the monarchy.

United as the Army of the Three Guarantees (independence, union, preservation of Roman Catholicism), the combined troops of Iturbide and Guerrero gained control of most of Mexico by the time Juan O'Donojú, appointed Spanish captain general, arrived in the viceregal capital. Without money, provisions, or troops, O'Donojú felt himself compelled to sign the Treaty of Córdoba on Aug. 24, 1821. The treaty officially ended New Spain's dependence on Old Spain, renamed the nation the Mexican Empire, and declared that the congress was to elect an emperor if no suitable European prince could be found. Although the Spanish crown initially rejected O'Donojú's recognition of Mexican independence, the date now recognized as that of separation from Old Spain is in fact Aug. 24, 1821. In one of the ironies of history, a conservative Mexico had gained independence from a temporarily liberal Spain.

# AGUSTÍN DE ITURBIDE

Agustín de Iturbide was a Mexican caudillo who became the leader of the conservative factions in the Mexican independence movement and, as Agustín I, briefly emperor of Mexico. He was born on Sept. 27, 1783, in Valladolid, Viceroyalty of New Spain (now Morelia, Mexico).

Like many young men of the upper classes in Spanish America, Iturbide entered the royalist army, becoming an officer in the provincial regiment of his native city in 1797. In 1810 Miguel Hidalgo y Costilla offered him a post with his revolutionary army, but Iturbide refused and pledged himself to the Spanish cause instead. His defense of Valladolid against the revolutionary forces of José María Morelos dealt a crushing blow to the insurgents, and for this victory

Iturbide was given command of the military district of Guanajuato and Michoacán. In 1816, however, grave charges of extortion and violence caused his removal.

By 1820 the radical independence movement was almost entirely extinguished. Both Hidalgo and Morelos had been captured and executed; only guerrilla bands (under the command of General Vicente Guerrero) prevented the complete victory of the royalists. The Mexican independence movement then performed a curious about-face. In reaction to a liberal coup d'état in Spain, the conservatives in Mexico (formerly staunch royalists) advocated immediate independence. Iturbide assumed command of the army and, at Iguala, allied his reactionary force with Guerrero's radical insurgents. Iturbide's Plan de Iguala, published on Feb. 24, 1821, proclaimed three guarantees: (1) immediate independence from Spain, (2) equality for Spaniards and Creoles, and (3) the supremacy of Roman Catholicism and a ban on all other religions. The Army of the Three Guarantees quickly subjugated the country; on Aug. 24, 1821, Juan O'Donojú, the new representative of the Spanish king, signed the Treaty of Córdoba, recognizing the independence of Mexico.

The revolutionary coalition quickly fell apart as Iturbide removed Guerrero and his insurgent following from influence. On May 19, 1822, Iturbide placed the crown upon his own head and became Agustín I, emperor of Mexico. An arbitrary and extravagant ruler, he proved unable to bring order and stability to his country, and all parties soon turned against him. Opposition solidified behind Antonio López de Santa Anna, whose own plan called for Iturbide's overthrow and exile. On March 19, 1823, Iturbide abdicated and went first to Italy and then to England. In 1824, however, he returned to Mexico, unaware that the congress had decreed his death. Captured on July 15, he was executed four days later. Although regarded by most scholars as a self-serving military adventurer, he has remained for the Roman Catholic Church and for the conservative classes the great hero of Mexican independence.

# THE MEXICAN EMPIRE

The first Mexican Empire spanned only a short transitional period during which Mexico became an independent republic. Independence from the former mother country had been the only glue that bound republicans and monarchists together, but, once that elusive goal had been achieved, the intrinsic animosity between the two came to dominate the body politic.

Iturbide first became president of a council of regents, which convoked a congress to draw up a new constitution. Deputies to the congress represented the intendancies. When

*AGUSTÍN ITURBIDE WAS CROWNED EMPEROR AGUSTÍN I ON MAY 19, 1822, BUT HE WAS FORCED TO ABDICATE LESS THAN A YEAR LATER.*

representatives from the Central American intendancies, part of the old viceroyalty of New Spain, declared that they did not wish to remain part of the Mexican Empire, they were allowed to withdraw and to organize their own governments.

On the evening of May 18, 1822, military groups in Mexico City proclaimed Iturbide Emperor Agustín I, and on the next day a majority in congress ratified the "people's choice" and recommended that the monarchy be hereditary, not elective. Agustín I was crowned in a pompous ceremony on July 21. The empire was recognized by the United States on Dec. 12, 1822, when the Mexican minister was officially received in Washington, D.C.

But even then Agustín's power and prestige were ebbing, and conflict soon developed between the military hero-emperor and the primarily civilian congress. On Oct. 31, 1822, the emperor dismissed congress and ruled through an appointed 45-man junta. The act, condemned by many as arbitrary, provided a pretext to revolt. Among the rebel leaders was General Antonio López de Santa Anna, who would dominate Mexico's political life for the next third of a century. In Veracruz, on Dec. 2, 1822, Santa Anna proclaimed that Mexico should become a republic, a position supported by many rebels and liberal leaders. Agustín was forced to reconvene congress and to abdicate. In 1824 he returned from European exile but was arrested and shot. This first epoch of independent Mexican national life foreshadowed many problems of the developing republic.

# CENTRAL AMERICA

The consequences of Agustín's overthrow extended from Mexico through Central America. Like the rest of Spain's empire, Central America had been affected by the French Revolution and subsequent Napoleonic Wars, despite revitalization of the colonial economy and of Spanish military strength under the Bourbons. The Kingdom of Guatemala—which included what are today the Mexican state of Chiapas and the nations of Guatemala, El Salvador, Honduras, Nicaragua, and Costa Rica—suffered hard times resulting from the disruption of Spanish shipping in wartime. Combined with locust plagues and competition from other producing areas, this caused a decline in indigo exports during the first two decades of the 19th century. The French invasion of Spain in 1808 increased the difficulties by adding burdensome taxes and demands for "patriotic donations" to support the resistance against the French; nevertheless, the kingdom remained loyal to the Spanish government at Cádiz during those difficult years. That government, ruling in the name of the captive Prince Ferdinand, made major reforms in an effort to maintain colonial loyalty and support. The Cádiz constitution of 1812 provided for colonial representation in the Spanish parliament and elections for municipal and provincial offices. These innovations triggered intense political activity, greatly increasing the importance of municipal and provincial councils.

A strong captain general, José de Bustamante y Guerra (1811–18), and Creole fear of Indian uprisings were factors that prevented Central Americans from seizing power as had been done in South America. The government easily put down such attempts in the state of San Salvador (which did not become El Salvador, the name by which it is now known, until 1841), Nicaragua, and Guatemala. In 1814, after the defeat of Napoleon, Ferdinand VII promptly annulled the 1812 constitution. This ungrateful act caused Creole opposition to Spanish rule in Central America to mount, especially against the repressive rule of Bustamante. The restoration of the constitution in 1820 once more permitted popular political activity in Central American towns and led to the emergence of factions that would form the basis of the liberal and conservative parties destined to dominate Central America for the following century.

A council of notables in Guatemala City accepted the independence plan of the Mexican Creole and former caudillo Agustín de Iturbide on Sept. 15, 1821, but there were wide differences of opinion among the municipalities on the next step. Some favoured independence from Mexico as well as from Spain, and some of the provinces also wanted independence from Guatemala. This divisive action by the municipalities was a product of their newly acquired vitality under the constitution, but it also reflected their resentment against centralized authority in Guatemala. Conservatives in Guatemala succeeded in annexing the kingdom to Iturbide's Mexican empire, but this led immediately to civil war, as San Salvador and Granada refused to accept the decision. Mexican and Guatemalan troops subdued San Salvador after a long siege, but in the meantime Iturbide's empire collapsed and was succeeded by a liberal republic that allowed Central America to go its own way. With the exception of Chiapas, these Central American provinces split off from Mexico in the wake of Iturbide's fall. They formed a federation, the United Provinces of Central America, which held together only until 1838, when regionalism led to the creation of separate countries in the region.

# BRAZIL

Brazil entered nationhood with considerably less strife and bloodshed than did the Spanish-speaking nations of the New World; however, the transition was not entirely peaceful. Like in Spanish America, Brazil was greatly affected by the Napoleonic Wars. Unique among colonies, though, was that events in Europe caused Brazil to serve as the court of its mother country, Portugal, for 15 years before gaining its independence.

## BRAZIL AFTER 1700

In the late 17th century the explorations of the Paulistas (settlers from São Paulo) finally led to the discovery of major gold deposits in a large district inland from Rio de Janeiro that

Engraved by Lester, from a Drawing by Craig.                    for the Gallery of Nature & Art.

MANNER OF WASHING FOR GOLD IN THE BRAZILIAN MOUNTAINS.

London. Published, by R.H.Rose, 45 Holborn Hill, May 1.1810.

*SLAVE LABOUR FUELED THE GOLD RUSH IN BRAZIL. IN THIS 1814 ENGRAVING, SLAVES ARE SEEN SEARCHING FOR ALLUVIAL GOLD, WHICH IS DEPOSITED AT THE BOTTOM OF A RIVER.*

became known as Minas Gerais. As the news spread, outsiders poured into the area. A time of turbulence, with the frontier Paulistas trying to assert their rights, ended after a few decades with the victory of the newcomers and the entry of royal authority. The south-centre, both the coast and the near interior, now took on the essential characteristics of the northeast—of a land living on European exports and inhabited by a population mainly Portuguese, African, and mulatto, with a large sector of slaves, along with many recently freed persons. The mining district flourished during the time of the boom, generating a network of settlements where none had been before and a local culture that included the now-renowned architectural style of its small churches.

More importantly for Brazil as a whole, Rio de Janeiro began to become an important urban centre in the usual mold, and the institutional component thickened, just as it had earlier on the basis of mineral wealth in the old Spanish-American central areas. By 1763 Rio had become the capital of Brazil, replacing Salvador in the northeast. Although the northeastern sugar industry continued to export more by value than the gold region, the latter had newer wealth and perhaps a higher profitability, and distant regions began to orient themselves to it in important ways. Stock-raising regions both in the northern interior and on the southern plains sent their animals to the mines, thereby both growing and helping unify the country.

The chronology of Brazil does not mesh closely with that of Spanish America in the late period. The gold boom was a type of development that had occurred much earlier in the Spanish territories; moreover, it did not last into the second half of the 18th century, when the most marked economic growth was occurring elsewhere, but began to decline by mid-century. Brazil had already experienced the bulk export revolution in the 17th century with sugar, and in the later 18th century exports were actually declining much of the time. Some growth, however, occurred late in the century in response to the decline of the French sugar industry in the Caribbean after the slave revolt in Haiti and some experimentation with new crops that were beginning to be of interest in Europe. Thus, though the Portuguese were as much affected by the Enlightenment as the Spaniards and had their time of active reform under the marquês de Pombal, prime minister and in effect ruler

# AGRICULTURE AND MINING

Brazil's society and economy were based on agriculture and mining, especially the export-oriented production of sugar and gold. The sugar industry, confined primarily to the Northeast, was the principal source of Brazilian wealth from the 16th to the 18th century, and it provided the crown with most of its revenue through the time of independence. Sugar production called for major investments in land, labour (*i.e.*, slaves), and machinery; consequently, a relatively small number of wealthy, plantation-owning families controlled the industry. Small landholders produced cotton and coffee, which became major exports in the 18th century. Independent freemen living near the sugar plantations raised tobacco and cattle, products that also became prominent by the end of the colonial period.

Colonists vainly sought gold in Brazil from the period of first settlement until 1695, when prospectors discovered large deposits in what is now the state of Minas Gerais. The subsequent gold rush rapidly changed the course of Brazilian settlement. Towns sprang up as if by magic in the hitherto unbroken wilderness while large sections of the coast were virtually depopulated. Slaves from Brazil's sugar plantations and Africa's gold-working regions, who were quickly brought into the region, introduced several mining techniques there. The gold mines had a huge impact on the Brazilian economy and brought such vast sums of money into the Southeast that the Portuguese government transferred the colonial capital from Salvador (in the northeast) to Rio de Janeiro in 1763. The search for gold led also to the discovery of diamonds in the early 18th century in Minas Gerais, Bahia, and Mato Grosso. The mining boom tapered off as the original deposits were depleted, although smaller quantities of gold and diamonds continued to be mined.

of Portugal in the period 1750–77, the context was hardly comparable. Outstanding among the actions taken under his ministry was a wave of expulsions of the Jesuits, in 1759.

During his long rule Pombal instituted numerous fiscal and administrative reforms and even attempted social legislation. He gave much attention to the far north of Brazil, attempting to develop the region, and a time of considerable local development and change did in fact coincide with his activity. He abolished the *donatário* system that had given land grants to favoured donors, granted legal rights to the Indians, encouraged immigration from the Azores and Madeira, created two privileged companies to oversee Brazilian trade, and established a monopoly over the diamond fields. Pombal expelled the Jesuits from Brazil and Portugal in 1759; many Brazilian elites endorsed the expulsion because the Jesuits had seemingly profited at their expense by resisting the enslavement of Indians and engaging in commercial ventures. Pombal progressively centralized the Brazilian government during the final decades of Portuguese rule.

# CAUSES OF BRAZILIAN INDEPENDENCE

Brazil gained its independence with little of the violence that marked similar transitions in Spanish America. Conspiracies against Portuguese rule during 1788–98 showed that some groups in Brazil had already been contemplating the idea of independence in the late 18th century. José Joaquim da Silva Xavier, popularly known as Tiradentes ("Tooth Puller"), instigated in 1789 the first rebellion against the Portuguese, who defeated his forces, executed him, and unwittingly made him a national hero in his martyrdom. Moreover, the Pombaline reforms of the second half of the 18th century, Portugal's attempt to overhaul the administration of its overseas possessions, were an inconvenience to many in the colony.

Still, the impulse toward independence was less powerful in Brazil than in Spanish America. Portugal, with more limited financial, human, and military resources than Spain, had never ruled its American subjects with as heavy a hand as its Iberian neighbour. Portugal neither enforced commercial monopolies as strictly nor excluded the American-born from high administrative positions as widely as did Spain. Many Brazilian-born and Portuguese elites had received the same education, especially at the University of Coimbra in Portugal. Their economic interests also tended to overlap. The reliance of the Brazilian upper classes on African slavery, finally, favoured their continued ties to Portugal. Plantation owners depended on the African slave trade, which Portugal controlled, to provide workers for the colony's main economic activities. The size of the resulting slave population—approximately half the total Brazilian population in 1800—also meant that Creoles shied away from political initiatives that might mean a loss of control over their social inferiors.

# THE PORTUGUESE COURT IN BRAZIL

The key step in the relatively bloodless end of colonial rule in Brazil was the transfer of the Portuguese court from Lisbon to Rio de Janeiro in 1808. This occurred as a result

**89**

of the French revolutionary and Napoleonic wars across the Atlantic. In 1807 Napoleon I invaded Portugal, a British ally, largely to tighten the European blockade of Great Britain. The Portuguese prince regent Dom João (later King John VI [João VI]) decided to take refuge in Brazil, making it the only colony to serve as the seat of government for its mother country. The prince, the royal family, and a horde of nobles and functionaries left Portugal on Nov. 29, 1807, under the protection of the British fleet. After several delays, they arrived at Rio de Janeiro on March 7, 1808. The colonists, convinced that a new era had dawned for Brazil, warmly welcomed Dom João, who promptly decreed a number of reforms.

The arrival of the court transformed Brazil in ways that made its return to colony status impossible. The unprecedented concentration of economic and administrative power in Rio de Janeiro brought a new integration to Brazil. The emergence of that capital as a large and increasingly sophisticated urban centre also expanded markets for Brazilian manufactures and other goods. Even more important to the development of manufacturing in Brazil was one of the first acts undertaken there by Dom João: the removal of old restrictions on manufacturing. Another of his enactments, the opening of Brazilian ports to direct trade with friendly countries, was less helpful to local manufacturers, but it further contributed to Brazil's emergence as a metropolis. Dom João installed in Rio de Janeiro his ministry and Council of State, Supreme Court, exchequer and royal treasury, Royal Mint, royal printing office, and the Bank of Brazil. He also founded a royal library, a military academy, and medical and law schools.

Brazil headed into a political crisis when groups in Portugal tried to reverse the metropolitanization of their former colony. With the end of the Napoleonic Wars came calls for Dom João to return to Lisbon. At first he demurred and in 1815 even raised Brazil to the status of kingdom, legally equal to Portugal within the empire that he ruled.

The situation was a difficult one for Dom João, who ascended to the throne as King John VI after his mother died in 1816. If he moved back to Lisbon, he might lose Brazil, but if he remained in Rio, he might well lose Portugal. A constitutionalist revolution began in Porto on Aug. 24, 1820; the revolution soon spread throughout the country and led to the formation of a junta in Lisbon on October 4. A constituent assembly was summoned that drew up a very liberal constitution, and the Portuguese demands became too strong for John to resist. In a move that ultimately facilitated Brazil's break with Portugal, John sailed for Lisbon in 1821 but left his son Dom Pedro behind as prince regent. It was Dom Pedro who, at the urging of local elites, oversaw the final emergence of an independent Brazil.

## THE BRAZILIAN EMPIRE

Matters were pushed toward independence by Portuguese reaction against the rising power of their former colony. Although the government constituted by the liberals after 1820 allowed Brazilian representation in a Cortes (parliament), it was clear that Portugal now wanted to reduce Brazil to its previous colonial condition, endangering all the concessions and powers the Brazilian elite had won. By late 1821 the situation was becoming unbearable. The Cortes now demanded that Dom Pedro return to Portugal. As his father had advised him to do,

*Don Pedro.*

*DOM PEDRO I WAS EMPEROR OF BRAZIL FOR MORE THAN EIGHT YEARS.*

the prince instead declared his intention to stay in Brazil in a speech known as the "Fico" ("I am staying"), and most Brazilians supported his decision. In January 1822 he formed a ministry headed by José Bonifácio de Andrada e Silva, a distinguished Paulista scholar later known as the Patriarch of Independence because he proved a tower of strength to the young regent during the first uncertain months of independence.

On June 3 Dom Pedro convoked a legislative and constituent assembly, and on September 7, on the plain of Ipiranga, near the city of São Paulo, he proclaimed the independence of Brazil. He was crowned emperor on December 1, completing Brazil's progression from Portuguese colony to autonomous country. The United States officially recognized the new nation in 1824, and the Portuguese acknowledged Brazilian independence the following year, whereupon other European monarchies established diplomatic relations. There was some armed resistance from Portuguese garrisons in Brazil, but the struggle was brief.

Independence still did not come without a price. Over the next 25 years Brazil suffered a series of regional revolts, some lasting as long as a decade and costing tens of thousands of lives. Dom Pedro I was forced from his throne in 1831, to be succeeded by his son, Dom Pedro II. The break with Portugal did not itself, however, produce the kind of disruption and devastation that plagued much of the former Spanish America. With its territory and economy largely intact, its government headed by a prince of the traditional royal family, and its society little changed, Brazil enjoyed continuities that made it extraordinarily stable in comparison with most of the other new states in the region.

# BUILDING NEW NATIONS

While Brazil maintained its territorial integrity after independence, the former Spanish America split into more than a dozen separate countries, following the administrative divisions of the colonial system. The difficulty for the inhabitants of these units was not, however, as simple as the demarcation of geographic boundaries. Rather, the recently emancipated countries of Latin America faced the much more daunting challenge of defining and consolidating new nations. With the structures of the old system removed, the inhabitants of each country set out on programs to create a postcolonial political, economic, and social order. The obstacles confronting them were myriad and imposing. As Bolívar himself exclaimed in a final cry of despair, "America is ungovernable for us…; he who serves a revolution ploughs the sea." Indeed, it was only toward 1850, at the end of a 25-year period sometimes known

THE BORDERS OF COUNTRIES IN SOUTH AMERICA AS SEEN IN THIS 1844 MAP ARE SIMILAR TO TODAY'S BOUNDARIES. NEW GRANADA LATER BROKE INTO THE SEPARATE NATIONS OF COLOMBIA AND PANAMA.

as "the long wait," that the outlines of that new order began to take their definitive form across the region.

# POLITICAL MODELS AND THE SEARCH FOR AUTHORITY

One of the most pressing and also most enduring problems that leaders of Latin American nations faced in the decades after independence was establishing the legitimacy of their new governments. In this regard the break with the colonial system proved traumatic. In Iberian political traditions, power and authority resided to a great extent in the figure of the monarch. Only the monarch had the ability to dominate the church, the military, and other powerful corporate groups in Iberian and colonial Latin American societies. Representative government and the concept of popular sovereignty, as a corollary, had a weak presence in Iberian political culture. With the Spanish king removed—and with him the ultimate source of political legitimacy—Creole elites had to find new foundations on which to construct systems of governance that their compatriots would accept and respect.

Although in practice they were unable to abandon the legacies of three centuries of Iberian colonial rule, leaders in Latin America turned generally to other political traditions for solutions to the problem of legitimacy. Adapting models from northern Europe and the United States, they set up republics across the region. Doing so not only helped justify their separation from Spain but also enabled Latin American elites to try to follow the example of countries they most admired, particularly Great Britain, the United States, and France. Many in the upper classes of Latin American societies identified political institutions as sources of the economic progress those countries were enjoying. At the same time, efforts to implement those political systems in Latin America brought different political ideas to the region's new countries: Enlightenment conceptions of politics based on rationality and a vision of politics as an interaction of individuals who enjoyed specific, definable rights and duties.

## CONSTITUTIONS

Particularly in the first, heady years of independence, elites throughout Latin America exhibited the influence of the Enlightenment in their propensity for producing constitutions. Those documents demonstrated not only attempts to impose rational plans on new nations but also the changing attitudes of elites toward their societies.

The earliest constitutions appeared in Venezuela, Chile, and New Granada in the years 1811–12. The authors of those founding documents rather optimistically intended to create representative government in independent Latin America and to declare inalienable natural rights of liberty, security, property, and equality. To implement those ideas, these constitutions set up a division of power in which the executive was comparatively weak.

From the mid-1810s to mid-century the overwhelming tendency was to move away from those early schemes. With different regions and elite factions battling against each other, the first liberal constitutional governments had failed. Now leaders in the region sought to erect stronger and more highly centralized states, again carefully laying out their programs in constitutions. This shift was not a rejection of foreign models. On the contrary, this change followed the evolution of European political thought; Latin American elites were now basing their ideas on different foreign theories, turning away from those of Jean-Jacques Rousseau and toward those of more conservative thinkers like Montesquieu and Jeremy Bentham. At the same time, the movement toward stronger executives and more centralized states reflected specific circumstances of these emerging new nations. At first, elites wanted a more powerful state to complete the victory over Spain and then to gain recognition from a Europe by this time dominated by antirepublican attitudes. As political order proved difficult to achieve, many Latin American leaders also looked to a more centralized state as an instrument against political and civil unrest.

Hopes for a new and stronger government only rarely centred on the idea of monarchy. Leaders in Argentina and Chile discussed the possibility of introducing a constitutional monarchy with a European king at its head. Mexico had emperors, first with Iturbide and then in 1864–67 with the Austrian emperor Francis Joseph's brother Maximilian, and Brazil enjoyed relative stability in a constitutional monarchy that lasted from independence until 1889. Still, such initiatives were temporary and exceptional. Latin Americans encountered a great deal of difficulty in finding suitable European princes to rule their countries. Local figures, furthermore, lacked the necessary authority to be accepted as monarchs. Thus, for practical as well as ideological reasons, republics were the rule during the 19th century. As leaders sought greater centralization, they adopted new forms of republicanism. Some, particularly military leaders such as Bolívar and the generals who had served under him, followed the model of a Napoleonic state. Bolívar's recommendation of a powerful president-for-life and a hereditary or life senate, resembling the structures of constitutional monarchy with republican ornamentation, was never followed. The predominant model was that of the regime that Spanish liberals had set up in 1812. Not all new constitutions after 1815 jettisoned federalism; Mexico in 1824, for instance, embraced that ideal. Overall, Latin America moved toward stronger, more centralized republican governments by the mid-19th century.

## DISORDER AND INSTABILITY

Written constitutions were not, however, sufficient to enforce order in the new countries of the region. Particularly in the 1825–50 period, Latin America experienced a high degree of political instability. National governments changed hands rapidly in most areas, which only prolonged the weakness and ineffectiveness of the emerging political systems. In Mexico, to take but one example, the years 1825–55 saw 48 turnovers in the national executive. Neither those in power nor those seeking office exhibited consistent respect for the often idealistic provisions of constitutions. In some cases the very authors of constitutions broke the rules laid out in them to gain or preserve control over governments. Like any other member of their society, they knew better than to expect their fellow political actors to stay within the strictures of the law. Extralegal maneuvers and the use of force became common elements of politics.

Much of the conflict that characterized these years consisted of simple disputes over power. Still, by the end of the 1830s

**99**

and into the 1840s, politics in many areas coalesced around two ideological poles, usually known as liberal and conservative. These groupings were not mass-based political parties in the 20th-century sense but rather factions of the elite; believing the majority of society to be ill-prepared for democracy, both liberals and conservatives intended to construct governments for the people but not by the people. Nonetheless, at times groups of artisans or peasant villagers took sides in the factional battles, hoping thus to press their own interests.

The precise definition of the sides in those fights is very difficult, owing to variations between countries and time periods. Urban merchants, rural landowners, and other economic interest groups overlapped so frequently—often within a single family—that it is impossible to generalize about the different origins of political factions. Moreover, the positions taken by one group could be surprising; in Venezuela in the 1840s, for instance, it was conservatives who supported free trade with the exterior, a stance that elsewhere was one of the classic tenets of liberalism. In general, however, one can say that liberals pressed harder for free trade and the rationalization and modernization of their societies—which essentially meant the adoption of European and North American liberal understandings of society as a collection of autonomous individuals. Conservatives, on the other hand, proved more favourable to old institutions, particularly the Roman Catholic Church, and to traditional visions of society as grounded in corporate groups. Indeed, in many contexts the question of whether or not to curtail the power of the church was the key point of divergence between otherwise similar liberal and conservative factions.

## MILITARIZATION AND *CAUDILLISMO*

To an extent, the role that violence or the threat of violence played in politics reflected a militarization brought about by the long period of the wars of independence. Only in Peru and even more so in Mexico did this phenomenon involve the continued influence of a regular, professional military class. Elsewhere the professional military failed to form a coherent interest group, and in many countries civilian politicians managed to control or even reduce the size of their national armies. It was rather in the power of militias and individual military leaders that the militarization of society was most visible. Throughout the region such forces grew to influence or even head national governments.

# PERSONALISMO

*Personalismo*, in Latin America, is the practice of glorifying a single leader, with the resulting subordination of the interests of political parties and ideologies and of constitutional government.

Latin American political parties have often been constituted by the personal following of a leader rather than by adherents of certain political beliefs or proponents of certain issues. Thus the popular term for such parties or their members has been often derived from their leaders—*e.g.*, Peronistas (the followers of Juan Perón, Argentine president in 1946-55, 1973-74) or Fidelistas (the followers of Fidel Castro, who led Cuba from 1959 to 2008). The archetypical demagogue and focus of *personalismo* in Mexico was General Antonio

(*continued on the next page*)

## PERSONALISMO (CONTINUED)

*JUAN PERÓN, AT THE MICROPHONE WITH HIS ARM LIFTED, SPEAKS TO A LARGE CROWD OF SUPPORTERS CIRCA 1950.*

López de Santa Anna, who dominated Mexican political life between 1821 and 1855. The Dominican Republic and Ecuador in particular have suffered from *personalismo*, but the phenomenon has been rather pervasive throughout Latin American history.

*Personalismo* is related to the phenomenon in Latin America called *caudillismo*, by which a government is controlled by leaders whose power typically rests on some combination of force and personal charisma (caudillos). During and immediately after the Latin American independence movement in the early 19th century, politically unstable conditions led to the widespread emergence of such leaders; thus the period is often referred to as the "age of the caudillos." The flamboyant leader of the independence movement, Simón Bolívar, was one such ruler (of Gran Colombia, his ephemeral political creation).

Although some nations, such as Argentina and Chile, developed more regular forms of constitutional government in the latter 19th century, *caudillismo* remained into the 20th century a common feature of Latin American states and prevailed in such countries as Argentina, during Perón's regime—as a form of political bossism—and in others as outright and brutal military dictatorship, as with the regime of Juan Vicente Gómez in Venezuela (ruled 1908-35). The latter was a ruler in the Venezuelan tradition, following the pattern of such strongmen as José Antonio Páez, who controlled the country in 1830-46 and again in 1860-63. Among other well-known caudillos of the 19th century were Juan Manuel de Rosas of Argentina, Francisco Solano López of Paraguay, and Andrés Santa Cruz of Bolivia. In such countries as Argentina and Mexico, during periods of weak central government, regional caudillos operated in their own localities in much the same way as did those on a national scale.

The military men who rose to positions of dominance were examples of the caudillo, a figure that epitomized this unstable period. Often coming to power through the use of violence, these leaders imposed themselves through the force of their own personalities, their control over armed followers, and their strategic alliances with elite groups. Some caudillos rose to power from humble beginnings, while others came from wealthy, landowning sectors and used their dependent workers as the core of their support. The stereotype of the caudillo as charismatic enough to win the enduring loyalty of his men and skilled enough to ride or fight better than any of them did not, of course, apply to all, but these were domineering and macho leaders. Whatever their social origins, caudillos in the postcolonial period became key political actors, working in alliance with, and at times under the control of, the economically powerful and civilian political leaders of the new nations of Latin America.

In a few cases caudillos contributed to political order. In Chile in the 1830s, for instance, the caudillo Diego Portales was a key figure in the establishment of a comparatively stable government. Allying with conservative elements, Portales helped found a political order that survived his death in 1837. It was an order based, as he put it, on "the weight of the night," meaning the ignorance and passivity of the popular majority— something he made little effort to change. Juan Manuel de Rosas, a caudillo who is said to have been able to outrope and outride his gaucho supporters, imposed a brutal political regime in Argentina from 1829 to 1852. Seeing his homeland split into partisan factions, Rosas sought to ensure a kind of peace by achieving the ultimate victory of one side. His iron-fisted administration, which made use of propaganda and a secret police force, pursued the interests of Rosas and his fellow Buenos Aires ranchers; still, caudillos from other provinces repeatedly tried to oust this violent leader.

Indeed, the very foundation of their power in personal relations and in violence meant that the legitimacy of caudillos' rule was always in doubt. Few were able to set up networks of alliances that could withstand the challenges of new leaders who emerged with their own armed supporters and wealthy allies. The system of *caudillismo* was a volatile one. Although the general type continued to exist throughout the 19th century, it was the postindependence period that represented the golden age of the caudillos.

# ECONOMIC OBSTACLES

Complicating the construction of stable, constitutional governments in the decades after independence were the economic circumstances that prevailed in the period. Creoles who had expected the dismantling of colonial restraints on Latin American economies to produce a wave of new wealth found their hopes dashed in the 1820s. In many ways the region's economies were poorer and less integrated in the first decades after independence than they had been in the late colonial period. Political disorder was both a cause and result of this situation. Unable to rely on old taxes for revenue and faced with military and bureaucratic expenses greater than those of the colonial regime, new governments commonly found themselves in tight financial straits. Their resulting weakness contributed to political instability, which at the same time impeded the reorganization of economic systems.

The wars of independence contributed to the disappointing postwar economic picture. In some areas, such as Venezuela, damage from the wars was extensive. Even where the destruction of human life and economic resources was less widespread, disruptions in financial arrangements and systems of labour relations provoked a decline in important economic sectors. Mining suffered particularly in many countries. The richest mineral producer, Mexico, needed roughly half a century to regain its preindependence levels of production.

As they emerged from their battles for emancipation, the new nations encountered other difficulties. The mere fact of political independence did not eliminate long-standing problems of transportation, but it did break down some traditional commercial networks. The entrance of foreign merchants and imported goods, although on a much more limited scale than

**105**

would later be the case, led to competition with, and in some areas the displacement of, local traders and producers. Apart from loans that left most countries in debt, the region received little capital from foreign sources. The departure of, or discrimination against, peninsular Spaniards reduced what had been a major source of skilled labour and administrative know-how, as well as capital for investment. Relatively few exports, such as coffee, sugar, and cattle products, found world markets favourable enough to stimulate the expansion of their production in Latin America. Colonial patterns had been destroyed, but the economies of the region had not yet found a consistent new orientation.

# SOCIAL CHANGE

The Creole elites who had headed the independence cause throughout Latin America had no intention of losing their social, economic, and political power in the construction of new nations. Managing to solidify and even expand their influence after the removal of colonial administration, these elites emerged as the great beneficiaries of independence, sometimes at the expense of other social groups.

## MOBILITY AND HIERARCHY

Leaders across the region quickly eliminated the system of separate ethnic castes. Persons of mixed race were, in theory, to have the same legal rights as members of the white upper classes. Indeed, the period of independence saw the ascension of individual mestizos and *castas* to positions of prominence. Service in the wars was particularly useful in this regard. Men such as the mulattoes Manuel Piar in Venezuela and José

Padilla in New Granada rose to the rank of general and admiral, respectively, in Bolívar's forces. In practice, however, the old hierarchies did not fall so easily and continued on informally. Those nonwhites who managed to achieve the status of elites were clearly exceptions to the general rule. The destruction of the caste system allowed for only limited loosening of racial and class hierarchies. Indeed, both Piar and Padilla were executed under rather questionable circumstances.

The position of Indians changed rather slowly in the postindependence era, despite some early and energetic

*THIS WATERCOLOUR SHOWS SIMÓN BOLÍVAR FREEING SLAVES IN 1816, ALTHOUGH MOST LATIN AMERICAN COUNTRIES DID NOT ABOLISH SLAVERY UNTIL THE MID-19TH CENTURY.*

initiatives. Spain had ended Indian tribute in 1810, and in the years after that several Latin American nations saw fit to repeat that measure with abolitions of their own. More generally, leaders frequently spoke of breaking down the barriers between the indigenous and more Hispanized sectors of their societies. Still, in the aftermath of independence, governments tended to reverse their positions toward Amerindian populations. The countries of the Andes, for example, reinstated Indian tribute, albeit under different names. Bolivian governments derived as much as 80 percent of their revenues from that source through mid-century. Full-scale attacks on indigenous communities' lands came later in the century.

Strong measures against African slavery similarly appeared in many areas by the late 1820s. Lawmakers declared the children of slaves to be free, banned the slave trade, or even ended slavery itself. Once again, however, there was a pattern of backsliding, so that, where slave labour played a significant economic role, the final abolition of the institution of slavery came about in most countries only about 1850. The growth of sugar production in Cuba and coffee production in Brazil, furthermore, meant that those two slave societies continued to flourish. Both areas continued to receive large numbers of new enslaved workers from Africa until after mid-century (1865 in Cuba, 1851 in Brazil) and only abolished slavery in the 1880s (1886 in Cuba, 1888 in Brazil).

## SOCIAL INSTITUTIONS

Both as part of their ideological commitment to liberal individualism and as a means of increasing the power of their new states, leaders in the postindependence years tried to establish their control over the formidable colonial institutions of the Roman Catholic Church and the military. Success came more easily in the case of the military. Only in Mexico and to a lesser extent in Peru did professional armies form fairly coherent interest groups pressing for the maintenance of their traditional privileges. After mid-century, however, those special privileges were lost even in these countries. The church, on the other hand, though losing a great deal of power, held on to a position of influence in much of the region. Armies of independence and some subsequent governments took over church properties and resources to meet their financial needs. In Buenos Aires and Montevideo, liberals were also able to trim the privileges of the church; elsewhere, however, attempts to do so either appeared later or, as in Mexico and Guatemala, provoked serious conflicts.

# LATIN AMERICAN RELATIONS WITH EUROPE

After ousting Napoleonic forces and reestablishing his monarchy in 1814, Ferdinand VII spent several years focusing Spain's military efforts on reestablishing rule over the Latin American colonies. However, a *pronunciamiento*, or revolt, in 1820 by the Spanish military against the king meant that Spanish efforts to mobilize a large army and fleet to send to America would never materialize. The continuing political disunity in Spain between liberal factions who sought a constitutional monarchy and the conservative reaction by those loyal to the monarchy and the church greatly weakened the Spanish response to developments in the American colonies. The liberal influences sweeping Spain also questioned the reestablishment of an antiquated empire greatly opposed to the liberal ideals for which the revolutionary generals in Latin America had fought. Furthermore, Spain found itself facing great economic difficulties in the wake of the Napoleonic War, and a costly reconquering of the Americas would have proven financially disadvantageous.

While Ferdinand and his advisers had initially scoffed at the idea of formally recognizing the independence of the new Spanish American states, the 1820s and 1830s became a period of sober realization that Spain would benefit from whatever economic advantage could be made from negotiating with the new political states. Yet, with the exception of those driven by the wave of political liberalism, the prevailing attitude in Spanish culture for years to come remained one of pride in Spain's imperial past. Spanish historians once again lauded the *conquistadores* and attributed any of the former colonies' successes to remnants of Spanish cultural influence. In fact, Spanish colonial law remained in effect in many regions of the Americas—in some cases even for decades. Spanish historians would come to see much of the anarchy and dictatorships that later came to the Latin American states as consequences of an independence movement that took hold prematurely without the long-term political or military strength to support itself.

Considering the unique circumstances that gave way to Brazilian independence, it is not surprising that Brazil's postindependence government and society were extensions of its politics and culture under Portuguese control. A constitutional monarchy led by Dom Pedro was established and remained in place as the form of government until a military coup proclaimed Brazil a republic in 1889. Meanwhile, Portugal became embroiled in a civil war known as the War of the Two Brothers to determine a rightful heir to its throne. As in Spain, disunity between liberal constitutionalists and conservative monarchists caused continuing political strife.

While Spain retained only a few colonies after the wars of Latin American independence, Portugal still possessed substantial colonial holdings. Brazil's independence in 1822 had left Portugal's overseas empire a largely African one, with scattered small holdings in Asia. By the 20th century, Brazilian-Portuguese relations had largely normalized, with the two countries sharing a special relationship due to their shared linguistic ties.

Former colonizers aside, the European nation that became most involved with the newly independent Latin American states was Great Britain. Both before and during the wars of independence, London had served as an important cultural hub for the revolutionary generals who eventually freed Latin America. Members of a volunteer force known as the British Legion had even fought and participated in many of the wars for independence under the leadership of Simón Bolívar. Longstanding tensions between Great Britain and Spain as competing world powers certainly motivated British volunteer militias.

Most notably, however, centuries of Spanish colonial mercantilism—an economic theory that, among its tenets, believes that all commerce between colonies and their mother countries should be a monopoly of the mother countries— had previously shut Great Britain out of the Latin American market. With Spain weakened by the Napoleonic War and engrossed in domestic issues, Great Britain took advantage of the opportunity to reap the commercial benefits of an open Latin American market. British influence in the region greatly increased, and Great Britain replaced Spain as Latin America's chief trading partner. Consequentially, Great Britain involved itself to varying degrees in the political developments of the new Latin American states, although for the most part it did not seek to establish its own new colonies there (with the clear exception of the Falkland Islands, taken in early 1833 from Argentine forces and possessed thereafter).

# LATIN AMERICAN RELATIONS WITH THE UNITED STATES

In 1822, the United States recognized the new Latin American states across Central and South America. But there was concern in both England and the United States that the continental powers would attempt to restore Spain's former colonies in Latin America, many of which had become newly independent nations. The United States was also concerned about Russia's territorial ambitions in the northwest coast of North America. As a consequence, George Canning, the British foreign minister, suggested a joint U.S.-British declaration forbidding future colonization in Latin America. President James Monroe was initially favourable to the idea, and former presidents Thomas Jefferson and James Madison concurred. But Secretary of State John Quincy Adams argued that the United States should issue a statement of American policy exclusively, and his view ultimately prevailed.

It is generally concluded that Adams was the sole author of the noncolonization principle of the doctrine; the principle of abstention from European wars and politics was common to all the fathers of American independence, inherited and expressed

*JAMES MONROE (STANDING), JOHN QUINCY ADAMS (FAR LEFT), AND OTHER MEMBERS OF THE CABINET DISCUSS THE MONROE DOCTRINE IN CLYDE O. DeLAND'S PAINTING.*

by the younger Adams all his professional life; in cabinet meetings, Adams also urged the dictum of nonintervention in the affairs of the nations of the Western Hemisphere. But Adams had no idea of proclaiming these dicta to the world. Monroe took responsibility for embodying them in a presidential message that he drafted himself. Modern historical judgment considers the Monroe Doctrine to be appropriately named.

Monroe enunciated his policy in his annual message to Congress on Dec. 2, 1823. Declaring that the Old World and New World had different systems and must remain distinct spheres, Monroe made four basic points: (1) The United States

# THE EVOLUTION OF THE MONROE DOCTRINE

When President James Monroe first issued his famous doctrine that the Western Hemisphere was closed to further colonization by European powers, the United States did not have the military power to back up his words. The United States did not invoke it nor oppose British occupation of the Falkland Islands in 1833 or subsequent British encroachments in Latin America.

In 1845 and again in 1848, however, President James K. Polk reiterated Monroe's principles in warning Britain and Spain not to establish footholds in Oregon, California, or Mexico's Yucatan peninsula. At the conclusion of the Civil War, the United States massed troops on the Rio Grande in support of a demand that France withdraw its puppet kingdom from Mexico. In 1867—in part due to U.S. pressure—France withdrew.

After 1870 interpretation of the Monroe Doctrine became increasingly broad. As the United States emerged as a world power, the Monroe Doctrine came to define a recognized sphere of influence. President Theodore Roosevelt added the Roosevelt Corollary to the Monroe Doctrine in 1904; it stated that, in cases of flagrant and chronic wrongdoing by a Latin American nation, the United States could intervene in the internal affairs of that nation. Roosevelt's assertion of hemispheric police power was designed to preclude violation of the Monroe Doctrine by European countries seeking redress of grievances against unruly or mismanaged Latin American states.

From the presidency of Theodore Roosevelt to that of Franklin Roosevelt, the United States frequently intervened in Latin America, especially in the Caribbean. Since the 1930s, the United States has attempted to formulate its Latin American foreign policy in consultation with the individual nations of the hemisphere and with the

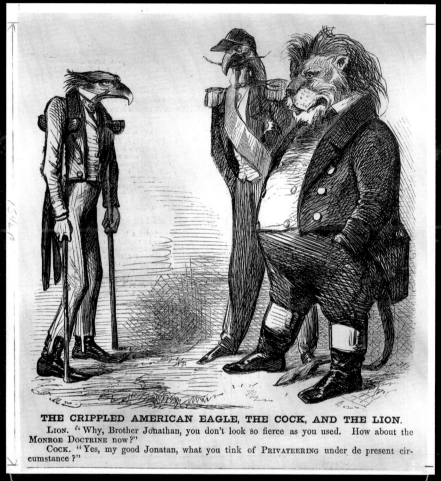

**THE CRIPPLED AMERICAN EAGLE, THE COCK, AND THE LION.**

LION. "Why, Brother Jonathan, you don't look so fierce as you used. How about the MONROE DOCTRINE now?"

COCK. "Yes, my good Jonatan, what you tink of PRIVATEERING under de present circumstance?"

*THIS POLITICAL CARTOON SHOWS FRANCE (THE COCK) AND BRITAIN (THE LION) MOCKING THE UNITED STATES (THE EAGLE) FOR BEING UNABLE TO ENFORCE THE MONROE DOCTRINE DURING THE AMERICAN CIVIL WAR.*

Organization of American States. Yet the United States continues to exercise a proprietary role at times of apparent threat to its national security, and the Western Hemisphere remains a predominantly U.S. sphere of influence.

would not interfere in the internal affairs of or the wars between European powers; (2) the United States recognized and would not interfere with existing colonies and dependencies in the Western Hemisphere; (3) the Western Hemisphere was closed to future colonization; and (4) any attempt by a European power to oppress or control any nation in the Western Hemisphere would be viewed as a hostile act against the United States.

The Monroe Doctrine, in asserting unilateral U.S. protection over the entire Western Hemisphere, was a foreign policy that could not have been sustained militarily in 1823. Monroe and Adams were well aware of the need for the British fleet to deter potential aggressors in Latin America. Because the United States was not a major power at the time and because the continental powers apparently had no serious intentions of recolonizing Latin America, Monroe's policy statement (it was not known as the "Monroe Doctrine" for nearly 30 years) was largely ignored outside the United States.

# 8

# THE
# POSTINDEPENDENCE
# STATES

The challenges that Latin America's former colonies faced as independent nations were complex. Brazil's government essentially remained an extension of its former monarchical system for many years before republican ideals would (forcibly) take hold. On the other hand, the independent countries of Spanish America, previously united by a common colonizer, became playing fields on which opposing political factors fought to exert control. With the forced uniformity of life under imperial Spain lifted, seemingly countless players stepped forward, and chaos ensued. The new nations struggled to create unity, national identities, and—as Bolívar had ominously predicted—stable political systems. In several states (notably Argentina, Venezuela, and Paraguay), the political chaos that followed independence was only reeled in by new forms of authoritarianism akin to monarchy, including dictatorships and *caudillismo.*

# ARGENTINA

After the postindependence dissolution of the former Viceroy-alty of the Río de la Plata, the remaining territory—what now constitutes modern Argentina—was frequently disunited until 1860. The root cause of the trouble, the power struggle between Buenos Aires and the rest of the country, was not settled until 1880, and even after that it continued to cause dissatisfaction.

In 1820 only two political organizations could claim more than strictly local and provincial followings: the revolutionary government in Buenos Aires and the League of Free Peoples, which had grown up along the Río de la Plata and its tributaries under the leadership of José Gervasio Artigas. But both organizations collapsed in that year, and Buenos Aires seemed to be losing its position as the seat of national government. However, as the city regained its function as an intermediary between the nation and foreign governments, it regained its prominence.

## DOMINANCE OF BUENOS AIRES

By then, military leaders had assumed power in almost every province. Each provincial political regime soon acquired its own character, according to the relative power held by military strongmen (caudillos) and by local political interests. This differentiation was not, however, cause for friction between the provinces; rather, economic and geographic factors separated them. Buenos Aires made significant advances toward national leadership by taking advantage of the interprovincial rivalries.

Within the province of Buenos Aires itself, the regime of the so-called Party of Order instituted popular reforms, including dismantling the military apparatus that had persisted from the war. The remaining armed forces were sent to defend the frontier areas and Pampas against attacks by Indians. This prudence on the part of the government won the support of the rural landowners as well as the urban businessmen, whose backing ensured victory at the polls.

The political order that seemed to be taking hold was achieved by setting aside, rather than resolving, certain fundamental difficulties. In particular, the institutional organization of the country was not carried out, and nothing was done about the Banda Oriental (the east bank of the Uruguay River), which was occupied first by Portuguese and then by Brazilian troops. By 1824 both problems were becoming urgent. Britain was willing to recognize Argentine independence, but only if Argentina established a government that could act for the whole country. And in the Banda Oriental a group of eastern patriots had taken over large sectors of the countryside and agitated for their reincorporation into the United Provinces of the Río de la Plata, forcing the Buenos Aires government to face the possibility of war with the Brazilian empire.

## PRESIDENCY OF BERNANDINO RIVADAVIA

In the meantime, an attempt was made to establish a national government through a constituent assembly that met in December 1824. Overstepping its legal authority, the constituent assembly in February 1826 created the office of president of the republic and installed the *porteño* (native of Buenos Aires) Bernandino Rivadavia as its first occupant. Civil war flared up in the interior provinces, soon dominated by Juan Facundo Quiroga—a caudillo from La Rioja who opposed centralization. When the assembly finally drafted a national constitution, the major portion of the country rejected it.

Meanwhile, war against Brazil had begun in 1825. The Argentine forces were able to defeat the Brazilians on the plains of Uruguay, but the Brazilian navy blockaded the Río de la Plata and succeeded in crippling Argentine commerce. Rivadavia, unable to end the war on favourable terms, resigned in July 1827, and the national government dissolved. Leadership of the province of Buenos Aires was given to a federalist, Colonel Manuel Dorrego. Dorrego was backed by local interest groups whose political spokesman was the great landowner Juan Manuel de Rosas, who had been named commander of the rural militia. Dorrego made peace with Brazil, and in 1828 the disputed eastern province was constituted as the independent state of Uruguay. The Uruguayan lands, which Rivadavia had considered indispensable to the "national integrity" of Argentina, were never to be recovered. In December 1828 troops returning from the war overthrew Dorrego and installed General Juan Lavalle in his place; Dorrego was executed.

## DICTATORSHIP OF JUAN MANUEL DE ROSAS

Rosas served as governor from 1829 until 1832. Disagreements between his federalists and Lavalle's centralists continued, but Rosas returned to the governorship once again in 1835 under the condition that he receive dictatorial powers.

JUAN MANUEL DE ROSAS'S SECRET POLICE FORCE ENFORCED HIS TOTALITARIAN REGIME AND TERRORIZED CITIZENS.

Rosas's 17-year dictatorship, although professing to be federalist, was in fact centralist and noted for its law and order through tyranny. His spies and the Mazorca, a ruthless secret police force, intimidated all opposition, so that by 1840 few dared to oppose him. He also ordered the display of his portrait in public places and churches as a sign of his supreme command. Finally a coalition of Brazilians, Uruguayans, and native Argentinians, under the leadership of Justo José de Urquiza, overthrew Rosas at the Battle of Caseros (Feb. 3, 1852). Rosas was forced to flee to England, where he spent the last years of his life as a farmer.

# PARAGUAY

Upon Paraguay's formal independence in 1813, a consulate of two men, militia captain Fulgencio Yegros and lawyer José Gaspar Rodríguez de Francia, was established to rule the republic for a year. At the end of that year, a new congress met and proclaimed Francia supreme dictator of the republic for a period of five years. In 1816 a third congress made him perpetual dictator, and his will was the law in Paraguay for an additional 24 years.

El Supremo, as he was known, prohibited any political activity, stripped the church of its holdings and power, confiscated the wealth of the small Spanish elite, and abolished the municipal government of Asunción. His policies generally isolated Paraguay from its rather hostile neighbours, even though the country's only tie to the outer world lay on the river route through Buenos Aires. In 1820 El Supremo found out about a plot to depose him and restore the native elite to power. Hundreds of arrests were made, and in the following year at least 68 men of the traditional Paraguayan aristocracy (including Fulgencio Yegros) were executed. Their wealth in land and slaves became part of the national patrimony, and well before Francia's death (1840) the state came to own a vast proportion of the country. With the borders sealed, Paraguay became of necessity almost self-sufficient; only a small, carefully regulated commerce was permitted with Argentina and Brazil. Uninvited foreigners were often held for years under loose arrest in the interior. Francia was a frugal and honest ruler but unspeakably cruel. The nation survived at a primitive level of self-sufficiency but at a terrible cost in political liberty.

When Francia died, he left behind a quietly prosperous country that had adjusted well to what amounted to state socialism, but he also left a country of rustics with no political experience and a strong tradition of dictatorial rule. In 1841 a second consulate emerged from the chaos in the figures of a civilian, Carlos Antonio López, and a soldier, Mariano Roque Alonso. It was soon clear that López was the true ruler of Paraguay, and in 1844 a congress named him president. The same congress promulgated a constitution, notable for the great powers accorded the president and the absence of the word "liberty" from its text. López devoted much of his two decades in power to opening the country slowly to the wider world and to modernization. Doing so provoked international crises, and it was not until after the fall of the Argentine dictator Juan Manuel de Rosas in 1852 that Argentina recognized Paraguayan sovereignty and eased its stranglehold on the rivers leading to the sea.

# CHILE

Chile was free as of 1818, but its inherent weaknesses were everywhere manifest. The Creoles remained bitterly divided between Bernardo O'Higgins and the Carreras. Two of the Carrera brothers had been executed in Mendoza, Argentina, in 1818; and José Miguel Carrera suffered the same fate in the same city in 1821. The elite groups were dedicated to the retention of those institutions on which such things as law, property, family,

*BERNANDO O'HIGGINS ABDICATED AS DICTATOR OF CHILE ON JANUARY 28, 1823.*

and religion were founded. The masses, who had been little more than spectators in the conflicts between 1810 and 1818, were excluded from government.

O'Higgins ruled as supreme dictator beginning in 1817. He created a working governmental organization and provided the essentials of the new nation—peace and order. Under adverse circumstances he succeeded in building a national navy and in mounting a major military expedition against Peru to fight the royalists. However, the Chilean oligarchy had little sympathy with O'Higgins, who favoured reducing their privileges. They accepted him, however, because he was supported by the army and because of dangers posed by Spaniards still in Peru and in parts of Chile (Valdivia and the island of Chiloé) and by internal guerrillas loyal to the Spanish monarchy. Opposition to O'Higgins began to make itself heard once the Chilean-Argentine army expelled the Spaniards from Peru; it increased after 1822, when the Chileans succeeded in driving the remaining Spaniards from Chile. O'Higgins's attempt, by means of a new constitution, to concede a larger political role to the oligarchy did not increase his support, and general unrest and poor harvests forced him to abdicate in 1823.

The years 1823–30 were troubled by an internal political split between the oligarchy and the army; 30 successive governments held office, and a variety of political experiments were tried. Rivalries developed between federalists and centralizers and between authoritarians and liberals. To the political chaos were added financial and economic disorder and an increase in lawlessness that tended to strengthen the authoritarian members of the oligarchy. Rival political factions were eliminated in 1829 when authoritarians, with the help of a part of the army, were able to install a junta (collegial government) that nominated José Tomás de Ovalle as provisory president. Actual power, however, was held by Diego Portales, who, as either a cabinet member or a private citizen, in fact ruled as a virtual dictator.

During the next 30 years, Chile established its own definitive organization, made possible by a compromise

*Sucre, the judicial capital of Bolivia, was named after the nation's first president, Antonio José de Sucre. This monument to him stands in Plaza 25 de Mayo.*

among the members of the oligarchy. Portales played an important role in the compromise, and a new constitution achieved as a result (1833) remained the basis of Chilean political life until 1925. It created a strong central government, responsive to the influence of the landowning class, which controlled the parliament.

The establishment of this new political structure united the different factions that brought Ovalle and later Joaquín Prieto to power. The new government was strengthened by a successful war against the Peruvian-Bolivian Confederation (1836–39), during which it broadened its support by reinstating army officers ousted when the conservatives had seized power in 1829–30.

During the next 30 years, Chile established its own definitive organization, made possible by a compromise among the members of the oligarchy. Portales played an important role in the compromise, and a new constitution achieved as a result (1833) remained the basis of Chilean political life until 1925. It created a strong central government, responsive to the influence of the landowning class, which controlled the parliament.

# BOLIVIA

In recognition of Simón Bolívar's support in liberating Upper Peru from Spanish control in 1825, congressional leaders named the new republic Bolivia in his honour, and they invited Antonio José de Sucre, his chief aide, to be the first president.

The new republic was not as viable as its leaders had fervently hoped it would be. Its economic growth was stunted, despite the region's immense mineral wealth and its historical prominence, because the decline in mining during the 18th century had given way to severe depression resulting from the wars of independence. Between 1803 and 1825 silver production at Potosí declined by more than 80 percent, and, by the time the first national census was taken in 1846, the republic listed more than 10,000 abandoned mines.

Bolivia became known as one of the more backward of the new republics. It rapidly lost its economic standing within Spanish America to such previously marginal areas as the Río de la Plata region and Chile, which were forging ahead on the basis of meat and cereal production. Bolivia, on the other hand, was a net importer of basic foods, even those consumed exclusively by its Indian population. The Bolivian republic, with little trade to tax and few resources to export, instead relied on direct taxation of its Indian peasant masses, who made up more than two-thirds of the estimated 1,100,000 population in 1825. This regressive form of taxation was a major source of revenue until the last quarter of the 19th century.

Economic decline was mirrored by political conflicts and a disregard for democratic principles. Bolivia emerged with a series of caudillos, among whom was Marshal Andrés de Santa Cruz, president from 1829 to 1839. Santa Cruz temporarily reorganized state finances in an effort to repair the war-torn economy, and he pursued policies of territorial expansion. In the 1830s he overthrew the Lima regime of General Agustín Gamarra and united Bolivia and Peru into a short-lived government known as the Confederation (1836–39). A combined force of Chileans and nationalistic Peruvians destroyed the Confederation, however, and Bolivia quickly turned in upon itself, abandoning further thoughts of regional dominance.

# PERU

The end of Spanish rule did not provide a solution to the many political, social, and economic problems facing Peru. The transition from a colonial dependency to a modern state proved difficult.

At the outset of Peru's national existence, caudillos who had gained prominence in the struggle for independence sought to seize power. The departure of Bolívar in 1826 removed a stabilizing influence. The aims of the caudillos were furthered by the absence of a tradition of self-government, by the prevalence of a feudal society of Creoles and Indians, and by the reluctance of civilians to assume political responsibility. Despite military influences, a liberal constitution was adopted in 1828. This did not prevent General Agustín Gamarra from taking government power by illegal means. He was succeeded in 1835 by another self-seeking caudillo, General Felipe Salaverry.

The ambitions of Gamarra and Salaverry were thwarted by Andrés de Santa Cruz, a military commander of Spanish-Indian descent who proposed a confederation of Peru and Bolivia. For three years Santa Cruz, though born in La Paz, was backed by influential groups in Peru and maintained the political union. But his hopes were shattered at the Battle of Yungay in 1839 by a joint force of nationalist-minded Peruvians and of Chileans fearing a threat to the balance of power in the Pacific.

During the initial period of statehood in Peru, liberal and conservative parties with ill-defined programs emerged. Their rivalry exacerbated the political instability of the country.

**129**

# URUGUAY

Uruguay did not become a separate state until 1828, and its first years of independence were disastrous. Twenty years of war and depredation had greatly reduced cattle numbers, and the lands and fortunes of many colonial families had been destroyed. Both Argentina and Brazil still coveted Uruguay. The factions of the first and second presidents, José Fructuoso Rivera and Manuel Oribe, battled each other in what became known as the Guerra Grande ("Great War"). Oribe's adherents, who displayed white colours, became the Blanco ("White") Party and controlled the interior. Rivera and his followers used red colours and became the Colorado ("Red") Party, based in Montevideo. The Blancos, supported by armies of the Argentine dictator Juan Manuel de Rosas, besieged Montevideo during the period 1843–51. The Colorados were aided first by France and England, then by Brazil.

When in 1851 the Guerra Grande ended without a clear victory for either side, the Uruguayan interior was devastated, the government was bankrupt, and the disappearance of an independent Uruguay had become a real possibility. Intellectuals wanted to abolish the political parties that had brought the country to such a low point, but the war had made too deep an impact on ordinary Uruguayans, who had become polarized into Colorados or Blancos. In 1865 the Colorados, aided by a Brazilian army, ousted the Blancos from power; however, the Paraguayan dictator, seeing that action as a threat to the regional balance of power, sparked the War of the Triple Alliance (1864/65–70), in which Brazil, Uruguay, and Argentina combined to defeat Paraguay. Uruguayan commerce was disrupted by the war, as well as by persistent political disputes, a civil war known as the Revolution of the Lances (1868–72), and Brazilian and Argentine involvement in Uruguayan affairs.

# COLOMBIA

After Venezuela and Ecuador seceded from Gran Colombia, New Granada (Colombia and the isthmus of Panama) was led by Francisco de Paula Santander from 1832 until 1837. Santander, the vice president under Bolívar and then leader of the opposition to Bolívar's imperial ambitions in 1828, was the dominant political figure of that era. The 1830s brought some prosperity to the new nation, but a civil war that broke out in 1840 ended a nascent industrial development, disrupted trade, and discouraged local enterprise. The seeds of political rivalry between liberals and conservatives had already been sown, and they bore fruit in the bloody revolution and costly violence that ravaged the country in the years between 1840 and 1903.

# VENEZUELA

After the destruction of the colonial system, Venezuela passed through an era of government-by-force that lasted more than a century, until the death of Juan Vicente Gómez in 1935. Backed by their personal armies, a series of warlordlike caudillos assumed power, which they exercised for their personal benefit rather than for that of the nation.

The first of the military dictators was General José Antonio Páez, who gave the country better government than it would see again for nearly a century. Bolívar had left Páez in charge of the armed forces of Venezuela, and he soon took full control of the country. He led the separation movement from Gran Colombia in 1829 and in 1830 convoked a constitutional convention for Venezuela. Páez dominated Venezuelan politics until 1848, both as president (1831–35 and 1839–43) and as a

*José Antonio Páez served as Venezuela's president twice and ushered in a long line of caudillos in that country.*

major political player. He subdued ambitious provincial caudillos and ruled in cooperation with the large landholders and leading merchants of the Conservative Party. The constitution that they enacted in 1830 reflected their social and political philosophy—a centralist state, property qualifications for voting, the death penalty for political crimes, guarantees for the freedom of trade and commerce, and the continuation of slavery. The church lost its tax immunity and its educational monopoly, and the army was shorn of its autonomy; thus, state supremacy was achieved. The government then began to reconstruct the war-torn economy by putting finances in order, establishing firm lines of foreign credit, and amortizing the national debt. It also constructed new roads to promote domestic commerce and facilitate coffee and cacao exports.

In contrast to the troubled times that preceded and followed it, the 1830–48 period of Conservative Party domination was an era of political stability, economic progress, and responsible administration. An opposition movement began to develop in 1840, however, when Antonio Leocadio Guzmán, the leading spokesman for dissident merchants and professional men, founded the Liberal Party. Guzmán's new liberal newspaper, *El Venezolano*, demanded abolition of slavery, extension of voting rights, and protection for the debtor classes. During the 1840s the demand for Venezuela's agricultural commodities declined on the world market; this produced economic difficulties, which in turn contributed to the increasing opposition to the Conservative oligarchy.

The growing political crisis was brought to a head in 1848 by General José Tadeo Monagas. Although elected president as a Conservative in 1846, he soon gravitated toward the Liberals. He intimidated the Conservative congress and appointed

Liberal Party ministers. When Páez rebelled in 1848, Monagas defeated him and forced him into exile.

# ECUADOR

Ecuador's early history as a country was a tormented one. An increasing rivalry and ideological differences between the Sierra and the Costa usually focused on the two leading cities—Quito, the capital, in the Sierra, and Guayaquil, the country's principal port, in the Costa. Quito was the home of a landed aristocracy whose positions of power during this early period were based on large semifeudal estates worked by Indian labour; it was (and to some extent has remained) a conservative clerical city, resistant to changes in the status quo. Guayaquil, on the other hand, by the 19th century had become a bustling cosmopolitan port, controlled by a few wealthy merchants. These men and those around them were influenced by 19th-century liberalism; interested in trade, they favoured free enterprise and expanding markets, and some were anticlerical. Their bourgeois attitudes conflicted sharply with the more aristocratic beliefs of the Sierra elites.

These early rivalries tended to be exacerbated by the nature of the two cities. The people of Guayaquil, the country's breadwinner and the home of Ecuador's industry and trade, felt that a disproportionate part of the state's tax income was spent in Quito by government bureaucrats. Those in Quito complained that their exports had to pass through the monopolistic bottleneck of Guayaquil, which acted as a traditional middleman and, by adding to the price of Sierra products, reduced their competitiveness in the world market.

Ambitious generals and politicians have played on this Quito-Guayaquil rivalry since the foundation of the republic in 1830. During the period 1830–45 two leaders from the wars of independence—Juan José Flores and Vicente Rocafuerte—struggled for power; Flores found much of his support in Quito, Rocafuerte in Guayaquil. Hostility was not constant, and for a few years the rivals agreed to alternate in the presidency. They were not simply personalist dictators; Rocafuerte in particular had a coherent ideology of government and did much to improve the educational institutions of the main cities. Both, however, were capable of deplorable conduct in their efforts to retain or regain power. Flores, on one occasion, even invited the Spaniards to return.

# MEXICO

Until they adopted a republican constitution in 1824, the Mexican people had little or no previous experience in self-government. Their economy was precarious: Mining, a mainstay in colonial times, had declined during the many years of fighting, and widespread anti-Spanish feelings had caused an exodus of Spaniards, depleting both the country's capital reserves and its pool of trained people. Political instability made borrowing abroad expensive, and nearly all public revenues had to come from customs receipts, which were pledged well in advance. As Mexico's national debt mounted, so did its problems, and it became trapped in a vicious, seemingly unbreakable cycle. Whenever public monies were insufficient to pay the army, its officers revolted, captured the government, and negotiated international loans. The high interest payments on such loans reduced available funds for education and other social and cultural improvements, which many Mexican leaders thought were urgent requirements.

The constitution of 1824 set a number of democratic goals and provided for a federal republic, consisting of 19 states, four territories, and the Mexico City federal district. Indigenous peoples lost their special colonial status, and accompanying protections, as wards of the government. In many ways they were worse off during the 19th century than they had been under the paternalism of the Spanish crown. In addition, restrictive state legislation excluded the great mass of peasantry from the political process. Because chattel slavery had greatly declined in Mexico and was less widespread than elsewhere in the Americas, a decree abolishing it in 1829 was largely symbolic.

Under various labels, two factions contended for control. The Centralists, who were generally conservative, favoured a strong central government in the viceregal tradition, a paid national army, and Roman Catholicism as the exclusive religion. Opposed to them were the Federalists, who favoured limited central government, local militia, and nearly autonomous states; they tended to be anticlerical and opposed the continuance of colonial fueros, which gave special status to ecclesiastics and the military and exempted them from various civil obligations.

The pendulum of power swung back and forth between the two groups. In 1824 Guadalupe Victoria, a Federalist and a leader in the independence movement, was elected Mexico's first president. Centralists replaced Federalists in 1828. A Federalist revolt in 1829 put Vicente Guerrero in the presidential chair, but he was soon overthrown by the Centralists, who held power until 1832. In 1833 another change placed Federalists in

*IN THE MILITARY AND IN POLITICS, ANTONIO LÓPEZ DE SANTA ANNA WAS KNOWN FOR FIGHTING ON BOTH SIDES OF ISSUES, CONTRIBUTING TO THE INSTABILITY OF POSTINDEPENDENCE MEXICO.*

power until 1836, when Centralists again regained control and held it for nearly a decade.

After the downfall of Iturbide, Mexican politics revolved for some time about the enigmatic personality of the charismatic Antonio López de Santa Anna, who seemingly had few fixed ideological or political beliefs. Allied with the Federalists, Santa Anna was first chosen president in 1833, but, rather than serve, he placed the liberal vice president, Valentín Gómez Farías, at the head of the government until Farías and his group in 1834 attacked the privileges of the clergy. Then Santa Anna assumed his presidential post and nullified the anticlerical legislation. Before his political career ended he would be in and out of the presidency 10 more times.

## CENTRAL AMERICA

On July 1, 1823, a liberal-dominated assembly elected from all the Central American provinces convened in Guatemala declared the independence of the former kingdom under the name the United Provinces of Central America. In 1824 it adopted the constitution of the Federal Republic of Central America, a document similar in its liberal features to the Spanish constitution of 1812, providing for a federation of Guatemala, San Salvador, Honduras, Nicaragua, and Costa Rica. Chiapas had elected to stay with Mexico, and Panama had become part of the Republic of Colombia in 1821.

However, the federation was short-lived, as tensions between the liberal and conservative groups led to civil war. In 1838, Nicaragua, Honduras, and Costa Rica seceded.

# UNITED PROVINCES OF CENTRAL AMERICA

The United Provinces of Central America was a union of what are now the states of Guatemala, Honduras, El Salvador, Costa Rica, and Nicaragua that existed from 1823 until 1840.

Since the 1520s these regions, along with the Mexican state of Chiapas, had composed the captaincy general of Guatemala, part of the Viceroyalty of New Spain (Mexico). In 1821 they became independent from Spain, and in 1822 they were joined to the ephemeral empire of Mexico, ruled by Agustín de Iturbide. Following Iturbide's abdication in March 1823, delegates from the Central American provinces, representing mostly upper-class Creoles, assembled at Guatemala City in July to declare themselves completely independent and to form a federal republic—the United Provinces of Central America. They drew up a constitution that provided for a federal capital in Guatemala City and a president for each of the five constituent states, which were to enjoy complete local autonomy; suffrage was restricted to the upper classes, slavery was abolished, and the privileges of the Roman Catholic Church were maintained. Manuel José Arce was elected first president in 1825.

Liberal-Conservative dissensions developed and soon erupted into civil war; the Liberals gained control in 1830, when their leader, Francisco Morazán, was elected president. His administration quickly disestablished the church and passed a series of anticlerical laws; other measures were enacted to promote trade and industry. In 1834 Morazán moved the capital of the foundering federation from Guatemala City, a Conservative stronghold, to San Salvador.

After an outbreak of cholera in 1837, which the clergy blamed on the "godless" Liberals, the Conservatives incited an Indian revolt. A mestizo rebel leader, Rafael Carrera, seized Guatemala City in 1838, whereupon most of the member states went their own ways. By April

(continued on page 141)

GROOTE MANNEN UIT DE GESCHIEDENIS VAN LATIJNSCH-AMERIKA
6. - RAFAËL CARRERA (1814-1865).
*Carrera leidt den opstand in Nicaragua.*
LIEBIG PRODUCTEN: nuttig en praktisch.

Nadruk verboden.

Uitleg op keerzijde.

*RAFAEL CARRERA WAS A RUTHLESS LEADER WHO FIRST GAINED POWER IN 1840 AND RULED GUATEMALA UNTIL HIS DEATH IN 1865.*

# UNITED PROVINCES OF CENTRAL AMERICA (CONTINUED)

1839, only El Salvador remained loyal. Morazán, after a disastrous defeat at the hands of Carrera in March 1840, resigned his office.

About 25 abortive attempts were made to restore the union. In the 19th century the Guatemalan government tried many times to gain hegemony over the other Central American states by force. Carrera, who controlled the Guatemalan government until his death in 1865, interfered frequently in El Salvador, Honduras, and Nicaragua by installing conservative regimes. Justo Rufino Barrios, Guatemalan president from 1873 to 1885, urged in 1882 that the old federation be revived; in 1885 he declared himself its ruler and marched his army into El Salvador, where he was defeated and killed at the Battle of Chalchuapa (April 2).

Rafael Carrera, a conservative who led peasant revolts that contributed to the federation's collapse, defeated the liberal Honduran general Francisco Morazán in 1840. Carrera quickly dismantled the liberal program in Guatemala and supported conservative caudillos in other Central American states. Although many entertained the possibility of reunification, all attempts failed, and conservative rulers in all the states opposed reunification.

Morazán returned in 1842 and seized power in Costa Rica, seeking to make it a base for restoration of the federation. He found little support for this and was himself ousted by Costa Rican conservatives and executed in San José on Sept. 15, 1842.

In 1847 Guatemala declared itself a sovereign republic and was quickly followed by Costa Rica in 1848 and eventually by the other regional states.

The alliance of Nicaraguan liberals with the American filibuster William Walker in 1855 caused Central Americans from all five states to unite against Walker, who made himself president of Nicaragua in 1856. In what became known as the "National War," this united army defeated Walker in 1857. Yet attempts to turn this effort into a new federal union gained little support from the conservative elites in each state; thus, the most lasting legacy of the conservative period was the fragmentation of the United Provinces into the five city-state republics. The middle of the century also witnessed strong British-U.S. rivalry in Central America for commercial rights and control of transisthmian transportation routes. Early 19th-century British commercial dominance later gave way to U.S. economic, diplomatic, cultural, and military dominance in the region.

# BRAZIL

The first decades of independence were difficult in Brazil, though not as chaotic as in Latin America's Spanish-speaking republics. Brazil underwent a series of regional revolts, some of which resulted in thousands of deaths, but the national economy remained strong and the central government largely intact. The emperor, Pedro I, who had declared Brazil's independence from Portugal in 1822, was impulsive, however, and made generally despotic and arbitrary decisions. In 1823 he dissolved the constituent assembly, which he regarded as unruly and radical, and sent Andrada e Silva and his two brothers into exile.

However, the emperor and his Council of State subsequently wrote a constitution that was liberal and advanced for its time, although it strengthened the hand of the emperor. The municipal councils debated and approved the document; Pedro promulgated it in 1824, and it proved versatile enough to last throughout the imperial period. The constitution helped centralize the government by granting the emperor power to dissolve the Chamber of Deputies, select members of the Senate, and appoint and dismiss ministers of state. Pedro I's popularity declined thereafter because he lost Brazil's Cisplatine province (now the republic of Uruguay) following a costly war with Argentina (1825–28), appointed few *mazombos* (Brazilian Creoles) to high office, overly preoccupied himself with Portuguese affairs, failed to get along with the legislature, and signed treaties with Great Britain that kept import duties low and exacted a promise to abolish the slave trade. As a result, Pedro formally abdicated on April 7, 1831, in favour of his five-year-old son, Dom Pedro de Alcântara (later Pedro II).

The next decade proved to be the most agitated period in Brazilian history. From 1831 to 1835 a triple regency tried in vain to end civil warfare in the provinces and to control lawless and insubordinate soldiers. In 1834 it amended the constitution to provide for the election of a sole regent to a four-year term; the document also partly decentralized the government by creating provincial assemblies with considerable local power. The priest Diogo Antônio Feijó, who was chosen as regent in 1835, struggled for two years to hold the nation together, but he was forced to resign. Pedro de Araújo Lima succeeded him. Many Brazilians were impatient with the regency and believed that the entire nation would rally behind the young ruler once he was crowned. On July 23, 1840, both houses of parliament agreed that he had attained his majority, though he was only 14.

# CONCLUSION

In the initial wake of the independence movements, the newly declared Latin American states struggled to develop political systems that could both be stable and also resist oligarchic tendencies, but the long run has shown that the wars of independence carved the path toward the formation of an autonomous and more economically developed Latin America. The late 19th century was by and large defined by the rise of export economies, which served to monetize the region's wealth of resources and draw the much-needed investment and technological development that had been so severely restricted during the colonial era. Manufacturing and industrialization correspondingly increased.

In the 20th century Latin America faced an array of both internal and external challenges, ranging from steady population increase to the consequences of the region's incorporation into the world economy. One of the most notable challenges has been Latin America's transformation throughout the 20th century from a largely rural society into the home of many of the world's most heavily populated urban centers. The societal problems spurred on by economic and urban development led at times to military juntas, Marxist guerillas, and foreign intervention—all of which served to divide segments of society and consequentially undermine the stability of governments or the public's trust in them.

However, by the end of the 20th century a revitalized commitment to democracy and neoliberal economics had brought Latin America to a new position historically—one that had been the goal of the revolutionary leaders in the wars of independence. Intra-Latin American free-trade arrangements moved forward too, with Mercosur (Mercado Común del Sur, "Common Market of the South")—which was organized in 1995 by Brazil, Argentina, Uruguay, and Paraguay—the most important. These trends toward greater cooperation and economic integration echo the sentiments expressed by Bolívar in the concluding paragraphs of the "Jamaica Letter." He writes, "Surely unity is what we need to complete our work of regeneration." While actively reinforcing the practical need for distinct political states, Bolívar predicted that Latin America would prosper most in its common goals by working as a collective force. It is how independence was achieved 200 years ago, and again in the 21st century it seems to be the brightest path toward regional regeneration.

# GLOSSARY

**AUDIENCIA** A court established to administer royal justice that served as an important governmental institution in colonial Spanish America.

**AUTHORITARIAN** Of, relating to, or favoring a political system that concentrates power in the hands of a leader or group not constitutionally responsible to the body of the people.

**CABILDO** A municipal council; the fundamental unit of local government in colonial Spanish America.

**CAUDILLO** A military dictator or strongman in Latin America.

**CONSERVATIVE** Of or relating to a political party, point of view, or philosophy that advocates preservation of the established order and views proposals for change critically and usually with distrust.

**COUP D'ÉTAT** A sudden decisive exercise of localized or concentrated force unseating the personnel of a government.

**CREOLE** Any person of European or African descent who was born in the West Indies or colonial French or Spanish America.

**FEDERALISM** Mode of political organization that unites separate states or other polities within an overarching political system in such a way as to allow each to maintain its own fundamental political integrity.

**GUERRILLA** Member of an irregular military force fighting small-scale, limited actions, in concert with an overall political-military strategy, against conventional military forces.

**HACIENDA** In colonial Spanish America, a large landed estate, one of the traditional institutions of rural life.

**IDEOLOGUE** A theorist, dreamer, or visionary.

**INTENDANCY** A colonial district ruled by an official who was directly responsible to the crown in Spain.

**JESUIT** A member of the Society of Jesus, a Roman Catholic order of religious men founded by St. Ignatius of Loyola, noted for its educational, missionary, and charitable works.

**JUNTA** A committee or administrative council, particularly one that rules a country after a coup d'état and before a legal government has been established.

**LIBERAL** Not bound by authoritarianism, orthodoxy, or traditional or established forms in action, attitude, or opinion.

**LLANERO** A cowboy or herdsman in Spanish America.

**MESTIZO** Any person of mixed blood; in Central and South America it denotes a person of combined Indian and European extraction.

**MILIEU** Environment or setting.

**OLIGARCHY** Government by the few, especially despotic power exercised by a small and privileged group for corrupt or selfish purposes.

**PENINSULAR** Any of the colonial residents of Latin America from the 16th through the early 19th centuries who had been born in Spain.

**PERIPHERY** The outward bounds of a region, as distinguished from its internal regions or center.

*PERSONALISMO* The practice of glorifying a single leader, with the resulting subordination of the interests of political parties and ideologies and of constitutional government.

**PROMULGATE** To issue or give out a law by way of putting into execution.

**PROVINCIAL** Of or relating to a province.

**SEDENTARY** Staying in the same place; not migratory.

# BIBLIOGRAPHY

## GENERAL WORKS

Leslie Bethell (ed.), *The Cambridge History of Latin America* (1984– ), is a general reference work with essays by recognized specialists on many aspects of the region's development. Edwin Williamson, *The Penguin History of Latin America* (1992); and Simon Collier, Harold Blakemore, and Thomas E. Skidmore (eds.), *The Cambridge Encyclopedia of Latin America and the Caribbean*, 2nd ed. (1992), offer introductory material. Tulio Halperín Donghi, *The Contemporary History of Latin America* (1993; originally published in Spanish, 1970), focuses on the region's colonial and neocolonial relations with North Atlantic nations.

Overviews of the colonial era are presented in James Lockhart and Stuart B. Schwartz, *Early Latin America: A History of Colonial Spanish America and Brazil* (1983); and Mark Burkholder and Lyman L. Johnson, *Colonial Latin America*, 2nd ed. (1994), both emphasizing analysis over narrative detail and treating all of Latin America as a unit. C.H. Haring, *The Spanish Empire in America* (1947, reprinted 1985), is an institutionalist classic. Sherburne F. Cook and Woodrow Borah, *Essays in Population History*, 3 vol. (1971–79), is by the field's most illustrious demographers. Asunción Lavrin (ed.), *Sexuality and Marriage in Colonial Latin America* (1989); and Lyman L. Johnson and Sonya Lipsett-Rivera (eds.), *The Faces of Honor: Sex, Shame, and Violence in Colonial Latin America* (1998), are anthologies.

John Lynch, *The Spanish American Revolutions, 1808–1826*, 2nd ed. (1986), is the best account of the political and military events of the wars for independence. Kenneth J. Andrien and Lyman L. Johnson (eds.), *The Political Economy of Spanish America in the Age of Revolution*, 1750–1850 (1994), compiles essays on economic aspects of the transition to independence. Robert H. Jackson (ed.), *Liberals, the Church, and Indian Peasants: Corporate Lands and the Challenge of Reform in Nineteenth-Century Spanish America* (1997), explores control and land-use reforms after independence. David Bushnell and Neill Macauly, *The Emergence of Latin America in the Nineteenth Century*, 2nd ed. (1994), focuses particularly on politics in the middle decades of the century. E. Bradford Burns, *The Poverty of Progress: Latin America in the Nineteenth Century* (1980), creatively argues that modernization hurt the majority of Latin Americans. John Charles Chasteen, *Heroes on Horseback: A Life and Times of the Last Gaucho Caudillos* (1995), is an exciting, highly readable study of two caudillo brothers and their divergent legacies in Brazil and Uruguay.

# ARGENTINA

An excellent historical summary is Thomas E. Skidmore and Peter H. Smith, *Modern Latin America*, 4th ed. (1997), chapter 3, "Argentina: Prosperity, Deadlock, and Change," pp. 68–113. Broader treatments can be found in Academia Nacional de la Historia, *Historia de la nación argentina: desde los origenes hasta la organización definitiva en 1862*, 3rd ed., 11 vol. in 15 (1961–63), and *Historia argentina contemporánea, 1862–1930*, 4 vol. (1965–67).

The colonial and early national periods are variously covered in Eduardo Crawley, *A House Divided: Argentina, 1880–1980* (1984); John Lynch, *Argentine Dictator: Juan Manuel De Rosas, 1829–1852* (1981); David Rock, *Argentina, 1516–1987: From Spanish Colonization to Alfonsín* (1987); James R. Scobie, *Argentina: A City and a Nation*,

2nd ed. (1971); and Ione S. Wright and Lisa M. Nekhom, *Historical Dictionary of Argentina* (1978). Susan Migden Socolow, *The Merchants of Buenos Aires, 1778–1810: Family and Commerce* (1978), is a prosopographical study. Jonathan C. Brown, *A Socioeconomic History of Argentina, 1776–1860* (1979), challenges assumptions about Latin America's economic dependence on North Atlantic powers.

# PARAGUAY

A general historical treatment of Paraguay is Harris Gaylord Warren, *Paraguay: An Informal History* (1949, reprinted 1982), with a useful bibliography. Barbara Ganson, *The Guaraní Under Spanish Rule in the Rio de la Plata* (2003), offers a revisionist view. The Francia period is addressed in Richard Alan White, *Paraguay's Autonomous Revolution, 1810–1840* (1978); and John Hoyt Williams, *The Rise and Fall of the Paraguayan Republic, 1800–1870* (1979), which also discusses the López dictators.

# CHILE

A historical overview is Brian Loveman, *Chile: The Legacy of Hispanic Capitalism*, 2nd ed. (1988). Works on various periods of Chilean history include Arnold J. Bauer, *Chilean Rural Society from the Spanish Conquest to 1930* (1975) and Simon Collier, *Ideas and Politics of Chilean Independence 1808–1833* (1967).

Jacques A. Barbier, *Reform and Politics in Bourbon Chile, 1755–1796* (1980), views all the governmental institutions of a single region as an interlocking unit, including their socioeconomic dimension.

# BOLIVIA

Overviews are provided by Robert Barton, *A Short History of the Republic of Bolivia*, 2nd ed. (1968); Herbert S. Klein, *Bolivia: The Evolution of a Multi-Ethnic Society*, 2nd ed. (1992); Charles Arnade, *Bolivian History* (1984); and *Waltraud Queiser Morales, Bolivia: Land of Struggle* (1992). Useful articles are found in Dwight B. Heath, *Historical Dictionary of Bolivia* (1972); and Barbara A. Tenenbaum (ed.), *Encyclopedia of Latin American History and Culture*, 5 vol. (1996).

Gustavo Adolfo Otero, *Life in the Spanish Colonies, with Particular Reference to Upper Peru, Now Bolivia* (1955; originally published in Spanish, 1942), provides information on the influence of Spanish colonization. Negative and positive approaches to Bolivia's history are represented, respectively, by Alcides Arguedas, *Obras completas*, vol. 2, *Historia* (1959), a dated but thorough history of Bolivia; and Carlos Montenegro, *Nacionalismo y coloniaje*, 6th ed. (1982). The complex reasons for the emergence of a separate independent Bolivia are given in detail by Charles W. Arnade, *The Emergence of the Republic of Bolivia* (1957, reissued 1970).

# PERU

General guides to Peru include Orin Starn, Carlos Iván Degregori, and Robin Kirk, *The Peru Reader: History, Culture, Politics*, 2nd ed. (2005); Jane Holligan de Díaz-Limanco, *Peru in Focus: A Guide to the People, Politics, and Culture* (1998); and *Country Review: Peru* (annual).

Enrique Tandeter, *Coercion and Market: Silver Mining in Colonial Potosí, 1692–1826* (1993; originally published in Spanish,

1992), facilitates comparison between the Mexican and Peruvian silver industries. Paul Gootenberg, *Between Silver and Guano: Commercial Policy and the State in Postindependence Peru* (1989), examines the complicated social contests through which integration into global economic relations emerged after independence. Florencia E. Mallon, *The Defense of Community in Peru's Central Highlands: Peasant Struggle and Capitalist Transition, 1860–1940* (1983), details the social and political aspects of a period of economic overhaul.

## URUGUAY

General overviews of Uruguayan history include Gerardo Caetano and José Pedro Rilla, *História contemporánea del Uruguay* (1994); Carlos Real de Azúa and Gerardo Caetano, *História y política en el Uruguay* (1997); and *Historia uruguaya (1974– )*, a comprehensive, multivolume work covering Uruguayan history from European discovery to 1958, published by Ediciones de la Banda Oriental.

## COLOMBIA

General works include Academia Colombiana de Historia, *Historia extensa de Colombia*, ed. by Luis Martínez Delgado (1964– ), a multivolume work covering all facets of Colombian history from precolonial to contemporary times, useful to the specialist; Robert H. Davis, *Historical Dictionary of Colombia*, 2nd ed. (1993), a convenient reference for people, events, and other aspects of Colombian history, with an excellent bibliography; and David Bushnell, *The Making of Modern Colombia: A Nation in Spite of Itself* (1993). David Bushnell, *The Santander Regime in*

*Gran Colombia* (1954, reissued 1970), covers the existence of Gran Colombia, 1819–1830.

# VENEZUELA

Overviews of Venezuela's history are found in Edwin Lieuwen, *Venezuela*, 2nd ed. (1965, reprinted 1985); J.M. Siso Martínez, *Historia de Venezuela*, 8th ed. (1968); J.L. Salcedo-Bastardo, *Historia fundamental de Venezuela*, 11th ed. (1996); John V. Lombardi, *Venezuela: The Search for Order, the Dream of Progress* (1982); and Judith Ewell, *Venezuela: A Century of Change* (1984). A recommended bibliography is John V. Lombardi, Germán Carrera Damas, and Roberta E. Adams, *Venezuelan History: A Comprehensive Working Bibliography* (1977). The evolution of U.S.-Venezuelan relations is examined in Judith Ewell, *Venezuela and the United States: From Monroe's Hemisphere to Petroleum's Empire* (1996). Donna Keyse Rudolph and G.A. Rudolph, *Historical Dictionary of Venezuela*, 2nd ed., rev., enlarged, and updated (1996), provides succinct information on major events and persons.

Specific events and periods are analyzed in Benjamín A. Frankel, *Venezuela y los Estados Unidos, 1810–1888* (1977), a fine account of 19th-century diplomatic relations; Robert L. Gilmore, *Caudillism and Militarism in Venezuela, 1810–1910* (1964), on the evolution from military personalism to military professionalism; Mariano Picón-Salas et al., *Venezuela independiente, 1810–1960* (1962), which includes essays on the evolution of society, culture, the economy, and the political system. Robert J. Ferry, *The Colonial Elite of Early Caracas: Formation & Crisis, 1567–1767* (1989), investigates society in a fringe area.

# ECUADOR

Colonial society and economy are engagingly described in Kris Lane, *Quito 1599: City and Colony in Transition* (2002). Suzanne Austin Alchon, *Native Society and Disease in Colonial Ecuador* (1991, reissued 2002); and Linda A. Newson, *Life and Death in Early Colonial Ecuador* (1995), provide detailed information on colonial demography. Erin O'Conner, *Gender, Indian, Nation: The Contradictions of Making Ecuador, 1830–1925* (2007), provides overviews of 19th-century history.

# MEXICO

Comprehensive surveys include Michael C. Meyer, William L. Sherman, and Susan M. Deeds, *The Course of Mexican History*, 7th ed. (2003); Michael S. Werner (ed.), *Encyclopedia of Mexico: History, Society & Culture*, 2 vol. (1997); and Colin M. MacLachlan and William H. Beezley, *El Gran Pueblo: A History of Greater Mexico*, 3rd ed. (2004).

Christon I. Archer, *The Army in Bourbon Mexico, 1760–1810* (1977), is a social-institutional study of the late colonial period. D.A. Brading, *Miners and Merchants in Bourbon Mexico, 1763–1810* (1971), is a massive social and economic study of Mexico's late-colonial international economy and government, and *Haciendas and Ranchos in the Mexican Bajío: León, 1700–1860* (1978), shows the rationality and market orientation of the agricultural sector. John K. Chance, *Race and Class in Colonial Oaxaca* (1978), studies urban demography. John E. Kicza, *Colonial Entrepreneurs: Families and Business in Bourbon Mexico City (1983– )*, broadly surveys urban society. Eric Van Young, *Hacienda and Market in Eighteenth-Century Mexico: The*

*Rural Economy of the Guadalajara Region, 1675–1820* (1981), links the growth of agrarian estates to the size and nature of urban populations. William B. Taylor, *Magistrates of the Sacred: Priests and Parishioners in Eighteenth-Century Mexico* (1996), studies the role of parish priests in New Spain. John Tutino, *From Insurrection to Revolution in Mexico: Social Bases of Agrarian Violence, 1750–1940* (1986), reviews rural rebels' motives from the wars preceding independence to those of the Mexican Revolution.

Studies of Mexican independence from Spain include Hugh M. Hamill, Jr., *The Hidalgo Revolt: Prelude to Mexican Independence* (1966, reprinted 1981); and Timothy E. Anna, *The Fall of the Royal Government in Mexico City* (1978). The difficult transition to nationhood is the subject of a valuable series of essays in Jaime E. Rodríguez O. (ed.), *The Independence of Mexico and the Creation of the New Nation* (1989). Barbara A. Tenenbaum, *The Politics of Penury: Debts and Taxes in Mexico, 1821–1856* (1986), is an economic history of the age of Santa Anna. Charles A. Hale, *Mexican Liberalism in the Age of Mora, 1821–1853* (1968), provides a model of intellectual history.

Studies of indigenous society include Charles Gibson, *The Aztecs Under Spanish Rule: A History of the Indians of the Valley of Mexico, 1519–1880* (1964), a large work based mainly on Spanish sources; William B. Taylor, *Drinking, Homicide & Rebellion in Colonial Mexican Villages* (1979), showing the relative normality of indigenous behaviour in central areas after the arrival of the Spaniards; Nancy M. Farriss, *Maya Society Under Colonial Rule: The Collective Enterprise of Survival* (1984, reissued with corrections, 1992), a broad treatment combining historical and anthropological techniques; and James Lockhart, *The Nahuas After the Conquest: A Social and Cultural History of the Indians of Central Mexico, Sixteenth Through Eighteenth Centuries* (1992), based largely on sources in Nahuatl.

# CENTRAL AMERICA

Ralph Lee Woodward, Jr., *Central America: A Nation Divided*, 2nd ed. (1985), is the standard English-language general history of Central America. Franklin D. Parker, *The Central American Republics* (1964, reprinted 1981), is still useful for its wealth of detail.

Murdo J. MacLeod, *Spanish Central America: A Socioeconomic History, 1520–1720* (1973, reissued 1984), is a thorough and well-documented history of the Spanish conquest and the Habsburg period. Miles L. Wortman, *Government and Society in Central America, 1680–1840* (1982), reviews the 18th-century history of the region and explains the impact of the Bourbon reforms on the region. Troy S. Floyd, *The Anglo-Spanish Struggle for Mosquitia* (1967), details the colonial rivalry for the eastern coast of Central America. Mario Rodríguez, *The Cádiz Experiment in Central America, 1808 to 1826* (1978), superbly studies the independence period and the influence of the Spanish constitution of 1812 in Central America. Thomas L. Karnes, *The Failure of Union: Central America, 1824–1975*, rev. ed. (1976), describes the failure of the Central American federation and surveys attempts to revive it throughout the 19th and 20th centuries.

# BRAZIL

Brazil's colonial past is detailed in Bailey W. Diffie, *A History of Colonial Brazil, 1500–1792* (1987), on the origins and growth of colonial Brazil; Leslie Bethell (ed.), *Colonial Brazil* (1987), seven interpretive essays; Kenneth R. Maxwell, *Conflicts and Conspiracies: Brazil and Portugal, 1750–1808* (1973), a significant interpretive study of the background to Brazilian independence;

and Caio Prado Junior, *The Colonial Background of Modern Brazil* (1967; originally published in Portuguese, 1942), a discussion of the predominant institutions implanted during the long colonial past and their impact on Brazil on the eve of independence.

Gilberto Freyre, *The Masters and the Slaves (Casa-Grande & Senzala): A Study in the Development of Brazilian Civilization*, 2nd ed., rev. (1946, reissued 1986; originally published in Portuguese, 4th ed., 2 vol., 1943), concerns the society of northeastern Brazil in the time of sugar production; most scholars today can credit very little of it, but it is read because it changed the direction of Brazilian historiography. A.J.R. Russell-Wood, *Fidalgos and Philanthropists: The Santa Casada Misericórdia of Bahia, 1550–1755* (1968), though nominally institutional, is tantamount to a study of northeastern urban society and partly updates Freyre. Stuart B. Schwartz, *Sovereignty and Society in Colonial Brazil: The High Court of Bahia and Its Judges, 1609–1751* (1973), combines social and institutional approaches, and his *Sugar Plantations in the Formation of Brazilian Society: Bahia, 1550–1835* (1985), embraces many methods, materials, and topics.

C.R. Boxer, *The Golden Age of Brazil, 1695–1750* (1962, reissued 1995), extracts a maximum of social, economic, and general information from institutional-narrative materials. Dauril Alden, *Royal Government in Colonial Brazil, with Special Reference to the Administration of the Marquis of Lavradio, Viceroy, 1769–1779* (1968), is broader than its title implies, dealing also with demographic and economic matters. Alida C. Metcalf, *Family and Frontier in Colonial Brazil: Santana de Parnaíba, 1580–1822* (1992), illuminates fringe-area society.

The imperial period is the subject of Gilberto Freyre, *The Mansions and the Shanties (Sobrados e mucambos): The Making of Modern Brazil* (1963, reissued 1986; originally published in

Portuguese, 1936), Roderick J. Barman, *Brazil: The Forging of a Nation, 1798–1852* (1988), and *Citizen Emperor: Pedro II and the Making of Brazil, 1825–91* (1999), thoughtful interpretations of the emergence of the nation-state. Emília Viotti da Costa, *The Brazilian Empire: Myths and Histories* (1985; originally published in Portuguese, 1977), collects well-written essays on liberalism, slavery, the end of the empire, and other major topics. C.H. Haring, *Empire in Brazil: A New World Experiment with Monarchy* (1958, reissued 1968), is a somewhat dated but still useful political history.

Warren Dean, *Rio Claro: A Brazilian Plantation System, 1820–1920* (1976), examines changing labour arrangements during the growth and demise of slavery. João José Reis, *Slave Rebellion in Brazil: The Muslim Uprising of 1835 in Bahia* (1993; originally published in Portuguese, 1986), weighs African cultural contributions and other factors in analyzing one of the century's most influential revolts. Stanley J. Stein, *Vassouras: A Brazilian Coffee County, 1850–1900: The Roles of Planter and Slave in a Plantation Society* (1985), studies the rise and decline of a traditional coffee zone. Richard Graham, *Patronage and Politics in Nineteenth-Century Brazil* (1990), analyzes the patronage system in the empire period.

## SIMÓN BOLÍVAR

An excellent Spanish-language biography of Bolívar is Tomás Polanco Alcántara, *Simón Bolívar: ensayo de interpretación biográfica a través de sus documentos* (1994). Biographies in English include the classic Gerhard Masur, *Simón Bolívar*, 2nd ed. (1969); and David Bushnell, *Simón Bolívar: Liberation and Disappointment* (2004). A penetrating study of Bolívar's ideas is V.A. Belaunde,

*Bolívar and the Political Thought of the Spanish American Revolution* (1938; reissued 1967). An abridged translation of the recollections of one of Bolívar's closest political and military aides (ends at 1826) is D.F. O'Leary, *Bolívar and the War of Independence* (1970). A slightly fictionalized biography of Manuela Sáenz is V.W. von Hagen, *The Four Seasons of Manuela, a Biography: The Love Story of Manuela Sáenz and Simón Bolívar* (1952). Sources of Bolívar's writings include *Simón Bolívar, Cartas del Libertador*, ed. by Vicente Lecuna, 12 vol. (1929–59), the most important collection of source material for the personality of Bolívar; and *Simón Bolívar, El Libertador: Writings of Simón Bolívar*, trans. by Frederick H. Fornoff and ed. by David Bushnell (2003), a useful introduction to the man and his image. Bolívar's widespread cultural influence is discussed in Christopher B. Conway, *The Cult of Bolivar in Latin American Literature* (2003).

## JOSÉ DE SAN MARTÍN

Bartolomé Mitre, *The Emancipation of South America*, trans. and abridged by William Pilling (1893, reprinted 1969), examines the works of José de San Martín during the time of South America's wars for independence. Biographies of San Martín include J.C.J. Metford, *San Martín, the Liberator* (1950); and John Lynch, *San Martín: Argentine Soldier, American Hero* (2009).

# INDEX